the FRUIT

love joy peace

of the SPIRIT

longsuffering gentleness goodness

of JESUS

faithfulness meekness temperance

CHRIST

**Reformed Free Publishing
Association**
Jenison, Michigan

the FRUIT

love joy peace

of the SPIRIT

longsuffering gentleness goodness

of JESUS

faithfulness meekness temperance

CHRIST

Richard J. Smit

©2012 Reformed Free Publishing Association
Printed in the United States of America

Scripture cited is taken from the Authorized (King James) Version

Psalter numbers cited are taken from *The Psalter with Doctrinal Standards, Liturgy, Church Order, and added Chorale Section,* reprinted and revised edition of the 1912 United Presbyterian *Psalter* (Grand Rapids, MI: Eerdmans, 1927; rev. ed. 1965)

Reformed Free Publishing Association
1894 Georgetown Center Drive
Jenison, MI 49428

The Reformed Free Publishing Association gratefully acknowledges the support of the Reformed Witness Committee of Hope Protestant Reformed Church in Walker, Michigan, in partial payment of the production costs of this book.

Book design by Erika Kiel

ISBN 978-1-936054-21-3
LCCN 2012920186

To my fellow saints of like precious faith
in the Philippines and abroad
"that ye should go and bring forth fruit,
and that your fruit should remain."

John 15:16

I am the vine, ye are the branches:
He that abideth in me, and I in him,
the same bringeth forth much fruit:
for without me ye can do nothing.

John 15:5

Contents

Preface

The Fruit of the Spirit of Jesus Christ originated from a series of sermons based on Galatians 5:22–23 that I preached for the customary applicatory worship services, following the Lord's supper worship services, in the Immanuel Protestant Reformed Church in Lacombe, Alberta, Canada, during my pastorate there from 2004 to 2009.

Of course, other Reformed books have been written on this truth of the fruit of the Spirit so that this book offers the reader nothing essentially new. Nevertheless, for those who might not have access to earlier writings on this truth, we trust that this book will fill a need for meditation on and instruction in the truth of the believer's life of thankfulness.

Hence the primary goal is that this material may promote faithful piety and godly living among God's saints that grow out of the doctrines of God's sovereign, particular grace, while at the same time giving due honor to the Holy Spirit, the Spirit of our Lord Jesus Christ, in the work of the sanctification and preservation of his saints.

Finally, we acknowledge with humble gratitude the commitment and guidance of the Reformed Witness Committee of Hope Protestant Reformed Church in Walker, Michigan, USA, to publish this material so that it can serve, among other needs, the need of a teaching tool for the Protestant Reformed Churches' mission labors in the Philippines about the Reformed believer's daily life of godliness and thanksgiving. May the Lord cause it to be useful to this purpose.

Chapter 1

INTRODUCTION

The apostle Paul warns us in the book of Galatians to avoid two extremes: the error of believing and living as though justification is by faith and also by and because of our obedience to the law and the error of believing and living as though our liberty in Christ is an opportunity to serve the lusts of the flesh. Instead of walking in either of these two evils of legalism or of antinomianism, we are called by the Lord to walk in the life to which he saves us.

What constitutes that new life in Jesus Christ and how that new life comes to visible expression in and through us is described, in one of many ways in Scripture, by Galatians 5:22–23. There the apostle teaches that our liberty and life in Jesus Christ become visibly manifest in "the fruit of the Spirit." That fruit of the Spirit, which he sovereignly works in the regenerated, believing, justified, and sanctified children of God, is "love, joy, peace, longsuffering, gentleness, goodness, faith, meekness, temperance."

I will examine extensively the fruit of the Spirit, considering in general the truth of the fruit of the Spirit in this chapter and then examining more closely each individual part in subsequent chapters.

The spiritual fruit evident in the child of God is the fruit *of the Spirit*. He is the Spirit of Christ. He in his sovereign power unites us to Christ in the living bond of faith. He took hold of us, who were dead branches in the dead tree of mankind, and ingrafted us into the living tree, Jesus Christ. Through that divinely established and maintained bond of faith, we receive the new life of Christ. Christ's purpose in joining us to himself by his Spirit is that we might bring forth fruit abundantly unto the glory of God.

Verses 22–23 of Galatians 5 emphasize the Spirit as the agent and worker of that fruit of the new life of Christ. He is sent into us by the Father and the word to bring to reality the covenantal bond between Christ and us. He is the one who sovereignly preserves and nurtures the bond by his almighty and irresistible grace. The Spirit brings us into that new life of the liberty of our Lord Jesus Christ. He raises us out of death into life. He calls us out of our darkness into his marvelous light. He joins us to Christ in the bond of faith and works that faith ... and a faithful confession of the faith. He applies to us the blessings of justification and as a result purifies us in the life of holiness and godliness. He preserves us daily until the day when we shall be like Christ in body and soul.

Unto that goal the Spirit then works in us his fruit. He works in and through us the production of his fruit. This work of the Spirit of Christ is not a cooperative effort between us and him. Rather, just as a grafted branch in an apple tree receives its life, nutrients, and support from the tree into which it has been grafted, so also our life, nutrients, and support come from the Spirit of Christ. We are his living and lively branches to bring forth much fruit.

The Spirit is pleased to work his fruit within and through us by dwelling in us. The Spirit comes irresistibly and breaks down the wall of enmity and pride of our dead hearts. He never waits for us to make the first move. He comes irresistibly into our hearts, and once there he remains in the new life of our regenerated hearts to work in us all things according to God's good pleasure. It is God's good pleasure that he causes us to produce spiritual, visible, holy fruit.

What is this good fruit, generally speaking? This good fruit can be described as the good works "which God hath before ordained that we should walk in them" (Eph. 2:10). These are the works that we perform out of the true faith of that living union to Christ, according to God's commandments and ordinances and unto the glory of his name alone. This fruit becomes evident in our confession and walk of life. This fruit is spiritually sweet and delightful not only to our Father in heaven, but also to our fellow saints. As a result of its spiritual pleasantness, our earnest desire is that Christ will work in us mightily by his Spirit this delightful fruit of his Spirit.

What does this fruit really look like in this life?

Galatians 5:22 teaches that this fruit is *one* fruit with nine different aspects. We do not read of fruits, but of *fruit*. The fruit of the Spirit can be compared perhaps to an orange. The orange is one fruit in our hand, but once we peel it open, we see that it has many distinct sections to it. Even though it has many sections to it, it remains one fruit joined together by its sweetness and goodness that fill each individual wedge.

Similarly, the Spirit produces in his living branches this delightful, covenantal fruit. A heavenly and spiritual sweetness and goodness characterize and permeate the whole fruit. Yet, the Spirit shows us in Galatians 5:22–23 that this one fruit has many distinct sections, which in their own unique way are filled with the spiritually delicious sweetness and goodness of the Spirit.

What is that delicious sweetness and goodness that permeates the whole of the fruit?

It is the love of the Spirit, which is mentioned first in the list of Galatians 5:22. The love of the Spirit of Christ is that bond of perfection, the bond in which we are knit to Christ by his Spirit and the bond in which he seeks us and takes us into the love-life of covenantal fellowship. That love of Christ is the unifying substance and sweetness that permeate the entire fruit of the Spirit. In this love we love God and the neighbor, which is in principle our whole life and duty in this new life and liberty of Jesus Christ. This love of the Spirit of Christ is fundamental to the joy, peace, longsuffering, gentleness, goodness, faithfulness, meekness, and temperance that the Spirit sovereignly works in and through us by his grace. That is the fruit that is delightfully tasty to our Father in heaven and also to our fellow saints upon earth who see and taste this fruit and are consequently delighted by it.

The Spirit is pleased to work this fruit in us through the way of leading us to crucify "the flesh with the affections and lusts" (Gal. 5:24). Those works and affections of the flesh are listed in verses 19–21: "adultery, fornication, uncleanness, lasciviousness, idolatry, witchcraft, hatred, variance, emulations, wrath, strife, seditions, heresies, envyings, murders, drunkenness, revellings, and such like." These works of the flesh work death and misery. Those who walk and continue therein "shall not inherit the kingdom of God" (v. 21). In that way one brings forth what is repulsive, rotten, bitter, and dead. While the fruit of the Spirit is unified and harmoniously full of goodness and sweetness, the works (notice the plural) of the flesh are divided, miserable, and bitingly bitter.

In that light we must regard our sinful natures as repulsive and evil. We must not view our lusts as something with which to play. We must not attempt to get as close as possible to the fulfillment of those lusts without actually falling into sin completely and getting caught in that sin. Rather, we must flee those works of the flesh like fleeing a plague of death. We must treat these works of the flesh as rotten fruit to be cast away.

This is the life of putting to death the works of the flesh and the sinful nature. It is a life of warfare against the lusts of the flesh. It is a life of daily seeking refuge at the cross of Calvary for the perfect obedience of Christ and for his strength to fight faithfully against our sins. It is a life of submitting to the word of God and willingly submitting to the knife of God's word to do its surgery on us: the slaying of our sins and wickedness and the building up of the faith and goodness of Christ within us.

We learn by the work of the Spirit in us that fruit-bearing does involve the painful process of being pruned from the works of the flesh unto the production of the fruit of the Spirit. Although the process is spiritually painful and grievous, the blessed goal is growing in the blessed life of producing the good fruit of love, joy, peace, longsuffering, gentleness, goodness, faith, meekness, and temperance.

Therefore, by the gracious wonder of the Spirit and grace of God, we are created in Christ Jesus to be bearers of the good fruit of the Spirit according to the measure that God has determined for the glory of his name.

To excite in us an earnest desire to see that the Spirit continues his work in us, we read in Galatians 5:23, concerning producing the fruit of the Spirit: "against such there is no law." It is not a crime to produce this fruit of the Spirit. The world may legislate against it. The world may persecute us for it. However, as far as the supreme court of God's tribunal is concerned, there is no ordinance in his law that states that we may not produce this fruit or that our production is limited strictly to a very meager quota. There are no human regulations, bylaws, or marketing boards that restrict or stifle fruit production. Never should there be a fear of over production.

Our production of the fruit of the Spirit falls within the realm of true Christian liberty. Just as it is the freedom of a rainbow trout to swim and to live within the God-ordained boundaries of its providentially appointed lake, so also it is our God-ordained and God-given life and freedom to produce the fruit of the Spirit according to his good pleasure and to the quantity that he has determined. It is our liberty to enjoy and bring forth this fruit of love, joy, peace, longsuffering, gentleness, goodness, faithfulness, meekness, and temperance. Therefore, you will find no divine law prohibiting you from pursuing that life of bringing forth the fruit whose sweetness and goodness are delightful to the Father and to your fellow saints. Rather, the Lord works in us and encourages in us by his word and Spirit the pursuit of daily fruit-bearing.

It is important that we seek in daily prayer that God by his Spirit may work in us the fruit of the Spirit. This is important because fruit-bearing is vital to the communion of the saints. By fruit-bearing, God is glorified among his saints. In our life of fruit-bearing, we are thereby assured of our eternal salvation. In this life of bearing forth the fruit of the Spirit, we are equipped to bear one another's burdens (Gal. 6:2) and to enjoy the liberty and peace of Christ with our fellow saints in the body of Christ.

As the Spirit works the beginning of that fruit-bearing within us in this life, we have blessed hope. It is true that our best works are polluted with sin. There appear on the fruit many spots of sin, and there hide in our best works worms of wickedness. But thereby the Spirit makes us long for the day when we shall be planted as living trees by the streams of living water that flow forth from the throne of God. There we shall bring forth abundantly, continuously, and sinlessly the heavenly, wholesome, pleasant, and sweet fruit of the Spirit of our Lord Jesus Christ for the honor and glory of our heavenly Father.

Questions for Discussion

1. Does the sovereignty of the Spirit of Christ in our salvation and sanctification mean that we are inactive?

2. Does the doctrine of sovereign grace make the believer careless and uninterested about the production of the fruit of the Spirit in his daily life?

3. What are the differences and the connections between calling and sanctification?

4. Why is it necessary for the believer to perform good works?

5. Prove from the word of God that God is the admirable author of our good works.

Chapter 2

LOVE

According to Galatians 5:22 the first of the nine parts of the fruit of the Spirit is love. Being first in the list does not mean that it is the first link in a long, loosely connected chain. Being first in the list means that love is fundamental to the whole fruit of the Spirit. Love is fundamental to the life of the justified and sanctified believer. Because it is fundamental and vital to our new life in him, Christ commands us to live in this love. In John 13:33–34, he said, "Little children... a new commandment I give unto you, That ye love one another; as I have loved you, that ye also love one another." He who by the working of the Spirit heeds that command of Christ and bears forth that pleasant fruit of love will then also be energized to bring forth the sweet fruit of joy, peace, longsuffering, gentleness, goodness, faithfulness, meekness, and temperance.

It is worthwhile to note that when Scripture speaks of the child of God and of love together, it frequently connects the two in the form of an exhortation. However, that is not so in Galatians 5:22. The Lord through the inspired apostle Paul does not exhort us to produce the fruit of love. The exhortation to love God and the neighbor may certainly be implied, but it is not explicitly stated.

What is the significance that Galatians 5:22 speaks of love as part of the fruit of the Spirit and as a spiritual reality in the sanctified child of God, but the verse does not exhort us unto that love? The absence of the exhortation reminds us that the love that the redeemed and renewed children of God must express to God and the neighbor is the fruit of the Spirit. This love is not our work; and its existence in our lives does not have its source in us, nor is its continued existence dependent or conditioned on us, our faith, or any of our works. The Spirit of Christ is the miracle-worker of the fruit-life in and through his people. The Spirit cultivates and nurtures the living branches who have been ingrafted by him into Christ Jesus. The Spirit is the agent of the Father and of Christ to work by his sovereign, almighty, and irresistible grace in his elect, regenerated people the fruit that God has foreordained that they must produce. When in this life we begin to learn and enjoy that fruit-life of love, that reality is not due to us, but it is the work of the Spirit. The Father, Christ, and the Holy Spirit receive all the glory and the credit for this wonder of the fruit-life of love appearing and being exercised in us and by us.

How does the Spirit cultivate and nurture that fruit of love in and through us throughout our lives? He cultivates and nurtures love by the means of grace: the preaching of the gospel and the administration of the sacraments. Powerfully and irresistibly the Spirit calls us unto newness of life. In the justified, he works by the means of grace to purify us unto the production of love. He turns us from the hatred of our old flesh and leads us forth into the love of our new nature in Christ Jesus.

Consequently, it is vitally important that we attend a church where the gospel of the Lord Jesus Christ is most purely preached and the sacraments are faithfully administered according to the ordinances of Christ. By the means of grace, the Spirit uses many passages in Scripture, including John 13:34–35, to work in us the fruit of the exercise of true love. By the living word of Christ, the Spirit of Christ cultivates, fertilizes, waters, and rigorously prunes us unto faithful production of the sweet fruit of love.

What is this fruit of love? True love is first of all love toward God. "I will love Thee, O LORD, my strength" (Ps. 18:1). True love is the spiritual activity of knowing Jehovah and delighting in him. It is the pursuit of fellowship and communion with the triune God in the knowledge of Christ Jesus. He that loves God desires to know him in all his glory and truth, especially as the God of his salvation in Christ Jesus. This is evident from the psalmist's confession in Psalm 18, in which he not only declares that he loves Jehovah, but also declares the reasons for his delight in communion with Jehovah: "The LORD is my rock, and my fortress, and my deliverer; my God, my strength, in whom I will trust; my buckler, and the horn of my salvation, and my high tower" (v. 2). For those glorious reasons, true love delights in God as our God in Christ Jesus and pursues blessed communion with him.

As the apostle John reminds us frequently in 1 John 3–4, we must love God, and we must love our neighbor who is brought providentially upon our pathway. True love for God is demonstrated in our love for the neighbor. Therefore, in 1 John 3:23, the apostle John declares, "And this is his commandment, That we should believe on the name of his son Jesus Christ, and love one another, as he gave us commandment." We learn that true love toward the neighbor seeks spiritual communion and fellowship in God and the Lord Jesus Christ. That is fellowship sought not in just anything, such as sin or false doctrines of men, but in a faithful confession of the name of Jesus Christ according to his word and the truth. This we must exercise toward one another.

Now, to understand the quality and character-istics of this love that we must exercise, the Lord in John 13:34 adds the sole standard of that love: "as I have loved you." Do you want to know what this love is that we must exercise toward one another? Look at Christ's love toward you. Have you seen and tasted that love? According to the standard of the quality, sweetness, and beauty of Christ's love toward you, so love one another.

As a result, what this love should be and how it ought to be exercised are not to be determined against the standard of what we feel like doing or not doing. We often attempt, and then fail, to exercise love in that way. Often our standard of love is whether it feels convenient or seems right to us in our own eyes. But that is not correct. The true standard that we are called by Christ to follow is clearly stated: "as I have loved you."

How did Christ love us?

He gave himself for us. He did not take anything from us except our guilt in order to satisfy God's justice for our justification. In all his work for us, he gave himself for us who by nature are nothing and totally unworthy. Even though while he died for us we hated him, yet he gave himself for us.

He loved us unconditionally. He did not love us because we loved him. He does not love us now because we love him. He will not love us tomorrow because we love him. He will not embrace us in his covenantal love only if we embrace or desire to embrace him first. We are not required to meet certain conditions before he seeks us and draws us unto himself. Christ loves us unconditionally.

He loved us entirely. He did not withhold from us part of himself. When he redeemed us by his complete sacrifice on Calvary, he did not hold anything back. He gave his heart, mind, and strength for us and to us. He even poured out his soul unto death for us.

Christ loved us faithfully. He never gave up on us half way or near to the end of his work of our redemption. It is not true that he loves us today, but tomorrow maybe he will not. His love was, is, and shall be unswervingly faithful unto us.

Christ loved us to the greatest extent of the required self-denial. He wanted not his will, but the Father's will to be done. Whatever was necessary for the salvation of his people, that was his will. Unto the fulfillment of that will of God, he denied himself totally.

Christ loved us with a purpose. His purpose was always our salvation. He did not love, except unto the salvation of the objects of his love. Those whom Jesus loved were those whom the Father gave to him from eternity. All those whom the Father chose in Christ, Christ loved unto the end of his earthly life on the cross. And such alone he continues to love with the purpose of their eternal salvation in glory with him.

Finally, Christ loved us with a holy love that was always consecrated unto the Father first. His love is pure. His love is sinless. His love was and always is in harmony with the glory of the Father. Because Christ loved and loves the Father, Christ loved and loves us whom the Father gave to him eternally. In his love unto us, Christ always has one eye of delight upon the glory of the Father.

As Christ loved us, so now must we love one another.

This does not mean that we can love entirely as Christ did. After all, Christ is our Lord and savior, and, as a result, it is impossible that our love could redeem ourselves or anyone else from sin and death. Furthermore, our love is rooted and totally dependent upon his redeeming love unto us. Although we may never attain to the glory and power of Christ's saving love, we must, nevertheless, pursue the standard of Christ's love in the new man of Christ. The love that is revealed in Christ must be a delight to us, and to imitate that love of Christ must also be our delight.

Is this an impossible standard for us to obtain? It certainly is for us. However, that forces us to see that Christ is not only the standard of this love, but Christ is also the perfection of that love that we must exercise to one another. Furthermore, Christ is the only and never failing fountain of that true love.

Since we are living branches united to Christ, our root and tree, in him we receive this love. Therefore, our desire must be that we produce this fruit of love out of him by the working of the Holy Spirit in and through us.

In that hope, we must love one another. We must love our spouses and our children, even in their most undeserving behavior. We must love our parents in spite of their weaknesses and faults. We must love our brothers and sisters in the Lord. In fact, we must love our neighbors, who can vary from time to time in God's providence. To such must we exercised the fruit of love.

Our love must give. It must not take and abuse for carnal and selfish motives. It must not give and expect that it be returned. It must forget self and deny self. As Christ gave himself for us, so we must give ourselves for the sake of others.

Love must not be exercised to one another only after certain conditions regarding the personality of the other person and how well he has treated us are first met. As Christ loved us, even when we were the least deserving of his love, so must we exercise the love of Christ toward one another.

Our love must be holy. Our love must not be carnal or motivated by lust or sin. True love cannot be enjoyed in the fellowship of sin and separation from God. Our love must be consecrated first to God and then to the neighbor according to God's word. As a result, true love will not compromise and stray into paths of sin; in contrast it maintains a clear view of the beauty and glory of our holy Father and the spiritual salvation of one another.

Oftentimes we face the difficult and practical question of how to love someone who does not live in daily repentance but walks in a sin. How do we love one who by his walk of life or denial of the truth shows that he hates God and Christ? How can we love such a person?

It is true that we cannot love the wicked in their sin. There can be no communion with the ungodly, and there may be no attempts for the godly to have spiritual fellowship with the ungodly (2 Cor. 6:14–18). There can be no true fellowship with the impenitent in his sin. Unrepented sin remains a barrier over and around which the ebb and flow of true communion cannot pass. Until sin is forsaken and there is reconciliation, there can be no true fellowship of love in Jesus Christ.

Hence, to love the wicked means that we may not tolerate their sins. We may not let the impenitent have the satisfaction of soothed consciences in the thought that we no longer are offended by what they consider to be just another way of life. In one way or another, we must address sinners and their offenses, which divide and separate them from full communion. The influence of our example, our conversation, or our attempts to call them to repentance should irritate and prick their consciences and force them to think about their sins and their duty to repent in the light of God's word.

In this way our love is both holy and purposeful. It is holy as God is holy. And it has the purpose to seek the repentance of the impenitent and their escape in Christ Jesus from spiritual ruin.

If the Lord so wills that the barrier of the offense is removed through the way of repentance and reconciliation, then communion and friendship may ebb and flow between two hearts joined in the Lord and in the peace of his shed blood. Therein will be enjoyed the sweetness of the fruit of true love as Christ has so loved us.

Let us seek the Lord earnestly in prayer for his grace and Spirit, in order that we may have this fruit of love more and more. What a delightful life and privilege it is to be the blessed recipients of the love of Christ and to love one another as he loved us.

Questions for Discussion

1. How does 1 John describe the fruit of love?

2. According to Psalm 139:21–22, may and must we hate others? Does this contradict Jesus,

who said, "Love your enemies" (Matt. 5:44)? How do we love our enemies while at the same time not compromising our faith?

3. In what practical ways should we show love to our parents, siblings, spouses, or even unbelieving neighbors?

4. How is one's love of an unbelieving neighbor different from one's love of a fellow saint?

5. While living in this virtue of love, can we ever hate?

6. How does 1 Corinthians 13 describe the fruit of love?

Chapter 3

JOY

Significantly, joy, one of the nine aspects of the fruit of the Spirit, is near the beginning of the list in Galatians 5:22, right beside love. Joy for the believer is not unimportant. The new life of Christ in us is one not of misery, but of spiritual joy. Even the wine of the Lord's supper signifies that the life that Christ works in us is not dismal and dark, but full of real, heavenly joy and gladness in him and with our fellow saints.

That joy is vital to the life of the believer is evident from Scripture. Since the Psalms frequently use the word "joy" and some of its synonyms, such as blessedness, happiness, and pleasantness, the Psalms teach that the believer's joy is a vital part of his life. Jesus himself speaks of the preeminent place of joy in our salvation. He said, "These things have I spoken unto you, that my joy might remain in you, and that your joy might be full" (John 15:11). The apostle John echoes the same esteem for the believer's joy in 1 John 1:4: "And these things write we unto you, that your joy may be full."

Wherefore, it is not at all strange that the apostle Paul exhorts the Philippians unto joy: "Rejoice in the Lord always: and again I say, Rejoice" (Phil. 4:4). We are exhorted by the Lord unto the production of spiritual joy.

What may seem strange to us, however, is the timing of this exhortation. The Philippians were in the throes of persecution. The church was despised by the world. She was in the crosshairs of the devil's rapid-fire cannon of temptations. It would seem that at that particular time in the life of the congregation, "rejoice" would hardly be the most appropriate admonition to give the people of God. The timing of this exhortation is very similar to that of Jesus when he spoke to the widow of Nain (Luke 7:11–16). She was on her way to the town cemetery where she planned to bury her only son. And Jesus said to her in her unimaginable grief, "Weep not" (v. 13). Is it appropriate that a child of God in such lowly circumstances be exhorted to produce the fruit of joy?

Such commands from the Lord are not out of place in our difficult times. We need to be called by Christ to rejoice in him. We need our heads lifted up unto the Lord and our hearts encouraged in the joy of our Lord. We need the Spirit of Christ to work in us this wonder-fruit of joy throughout our life, even in our troubles and afflictions.

According to the exhortation in Philippians 4:4, true joy centers in the Lord. There can be no true joy apart from the Lord. The world believes that there is true joy only apart from Christ. The world believes that joy and gladness can be found in the worship of false gods and in the wicked pursuits of covetousness, gambling, fornication, reveling, drunkenness, and the like. The world believes that real joy can be produced in a life of self-centeredness without God, Christ, and the word of God. However, the only true joy there is for the elect, regenerated, and sanctified child of God is the joy of Christ and his Spirit.

One can find examples in creation that illustrate the foolishness of the world's philosophy about joy and happiness. For example, God ordained that a fish enjoys its life and creaturely happiness within the God-ordained place of its lake. Within the boundaries of the lakeshore, the fish thrives. As soon as the fish attempts to escape its God-ordained boundaries and tries to live on land, it will die. Such a fish will learn by its untimely death that there is no life and happiness outside its boundaries.

Similarly, God originally put man in his proper place to serve God and to love God in holiness and righteousness. Within those God-ordained boundaries Adam and Eve thrived in perfection and rejoiced in their place in paradise with God. They had life and happiness in covenantal friendship with God and with each other in their marriage.

However, when man sinned, he forsook the God-ordained boundaries. He thought in his foolishness that there was joy to be found on the other side of the God-ordained boundaries. Like a fish that tries to live on land, so man living apart from God found in the fall only misery and death. Still today, wicked and unbelieving man will find only misery and death apart from Christ and his word. Although the world persistently portrays a life of godlessness and unrighteousness as joyful, such a life of the hatred of God is only misery and death.

As the psalmist David explained in Psalm 32:3–4, we learn through our falls into sin that there is no joy apart from the Lord. There is no joy for those who hide their sin and refuse to repent of it. There is no joy while walking in sin. No joy in a cover-up of our sin by a complicated web of lies and deceit. Instead of joy, there is for the unbelieving and wicked only "many sorrows" (v. 10).

The fruit of joy is found only "in the Lord." True joy has its only source in our Lord and savior, Jesus Christ, who himself is the joy of the Father in heaven. Christ was joyful while he performed the will of his Father. Christ counted it a joy to redeem his people from sin by his own shed blood. Christ rejoices in glory at the right hand of the Father. There Christ's desire is that we might share in his joy so that he works in us his life of joy.

That our joy is "in the Lord" includes the idea that our joy is experienced in fellowship and prayer with the Father in him. It is not true that the extent of our joy is merely that we understand our privilege to do the Lord's work here below, and then rejoice in that privilege and duty. "In the Lord" includes the idea that we count it all joy to belong to Christ spiritually and to know that he is our friend-sovereign who will never leave us nor forsake us.

Because our joy is only in Christ, we must not overlook the fact that true joy is a spiritual and heavenly joy. It is not temporal and fleeting. It is not the superficial joy of the charismatic movement. It is not mere emotional excitement. It is not a joy in which one feels good about himself. It is not even the joy of an ever-present, one-thousand megawatt smile.

Certainly, the true joy of the believer is not presumptuous, like the Pharisee in the parable of the Pharisee and the publican (Luke 18:9–14). The Pharisee in that notable parable prayed to God with joy in his heart before God. Nevertheless, his joy was not produced by the Spirit. It was a superficial, hollow joy that was rooted in his own works and sup-posed righteousness and, therefore, without a real foundation.

In fact, Jesus spoke of those who in the

judgment will say, "Lord, Lord, have we not prophesied in thy name? and in thy name have cast out devils? and in thy name done many wonderful works?" (Matt 7:22). Those who rejoice in their own works base their joy in themselves and their own righteousness. What a rude awakening such self-boasters will have when, as Jesus explained, they will be told by the judge in their judgment: "I never knew you: depart from me, ye that work iniquity!" Such shall be cast into everlasting sorrow and misery. To those who in pride and unbelief trust in their own works and righteousness, there is only sorrow.

Moreover, the true joy of the believer is not based upon earthly things. It is not based upon the quantity and the quality of their wealth and health. We may be tempted to think that if we receive much earthly prosperity and sound health, then we may be joyful in the Lord; but, when providentially we are given very little wealth and ill health, then there is no reason for joy. That is not the idea of the true, spiritual joy of the Spirit of Christ. The joy of the Spirit is not selfish, covetous, or carnal; but it is centered in the Lord, is full of contentment, and delights to do the will of the Father.

Finally, consider that true joy is not the same thing as common earthly joys that we experience. There are the earthly joys of our close, earthly relationships. There are the earthly joys of newlyweds, of marriage, of family, of children, and of grandchildren, which are even more enjoyable when we experience such things with those of like precious faith. But can those joys, which are good gifts of God and must be received with thanksgiving, be the true, lasting, spiritual joy of the believer, when they will pass away?

The true joy, which is the wonder-fruit of the Spirit, is everlasting and victorious. It is based upon the righteousness that Christ earned for all his elect for whom and whom alone he died and made a complete atonement. Our true gladness flows out of a true and living faith in the Lord Jesus Christ. It is filled with the substantial knowledge of the doctrines of the Reformed faith. The joy of believers is the knowledge and conviction of the truth of the triune God and his only begotten Son, their Lord and savior.

Additionally, that joy is the assurance of God's goodness and love toward us for the sake of Christ. That assurance includes the basic comfort that we belong unto him in body and soul because of the complete atonement by his shed blood. Because of that work of Christ, the Father delights in us, and we possess in Christ the life and experience of delight in him. That is the joy of fellowship with our bridegroom, Christ, reflected in the marital joy of a newlywed husband and wife, made one in the Lord. That true joy, which is rooted in Christ, transcends the vanity of this life and looks heavenward for the complete joy of our Lord. This is the lasting joy that we confess and sing in the last part of a familiar doxology: "Thus may we abide in union with each other and the Lord: and possess in sweet communion joys which earth cannot afford."

In this life already by the Spirit of Christ, we consciously learn and experience this joy according to our new nature. This joy is not a mere emotion, although it is often true that, because of this joy in the Lord Jesus Christ, we are moved emotionally. This is a virtue that is connected with the knowledge and conviction of our faith. Hence, as the Lord works this fruit of joy in us by his word and Spirit, we rejoice for knowable and worthy reasons. In antithetical contrast to all the sinful and self-centered reasons that the wicked world has for its fleeting joys, the child of God has many good, virtuous, substantial, and lasting reasons.

The primary reason for joy in our hearts is that God, whom Christ our Lord reveals, is great in his being, power, and majesty. Delight in God because he is God. Rejoice in the Lord Jesus Christ because he is God!

What is even more joyful is that the triune God for Christ's sake is our God! He is the God who dwells in Zion. He is God who is our guide even unto death!

We rejoice in the Lord, who is God the creator. By Christ, God made the heavens and the earth and all the creatures therein. God instantaneously, by his word and Spirit, made all things. By faith, the child of God delights in the glory of the living God that his handiwork displays day unto day. What delight it is to know that the God whose creation shows forth his sovereignty and omnipotence is our great creator.

We have joy because this God is the God of our salvation. We are his new creation in Christ Jesus.

We rejoice because, to make us that new creation of God, Christ has removed from us the curse due to our sin. We rejoice that Christ became for us the man of sorrows, acquainted with grief, feeling the weight and inexpressible anguish of the suffering of God's wrath, especially when it engulfed him on the cross. We rejoice that he became the man of sorrows so that we can be his joyful children.

When beholding the wonder of Christ's redemptive suffering for us, we rejoice to know that the Lord joyfully gave himself for us. Even in the darkness of being forsaken, it was his joy to do the Father's will, which required that hellish death on the cross for our redemption. That it was Christ's delight to do the will of God, even in that hellish hour, is evident when he cried out, "My God, my God, why hast thou forsaken me?" That word of Christ on the cross was both the fullest expression of his complete agony under the wrath of God for our sin and also, at the same time, the clearest expression of his obedience and joy to fulfill the Father's will. As he was made to feel the utter bitterness and misery of the curse for our sin, there were upon his heart the psalms of God, one of which he uttered upon the cross in the darkness (Ps. 22:1). When Christ came out of that second death, his joy was his God because he declared, "I thirst!" He thirsted for the living God! His joy and delight in his misery and humiliation remained in the Father. What a joy to know that because of Christ's redemptive joy and delight, we have righteousness in Christ before the Father through faith alone. Therefore, rejoice for the deliverance we have in and through Christ from the eternal misery of our sin and for the right we have in him to eternal joy with the Father.

Then we may rejoice that the Lord counts it all joy to come into us and dwell in us. The Lord does not remain far from us. He does not forget about us, nor does he regard our needs as a hindrance to his joy. Rather, he delights to dwell in us by his Spirit. He delights to work in us sovereignly and in his wisdom and good time by his grace what is beautiful and pleasing in his sight. Rejoice that he is the author and finisher of our faith. Rejoice that he is our wisdom, strength, and very present help in trouble.

This Lord who dwells in us by his Spirit is the Lord at God's right hand. He is seated in all royal power and authority. Before him shall every knee bow. All shall declare him to be Lord. What a reason for us to rejoice! Why? This truth shows that nothing in heaven or on the earth happens by chance, but that all things in our present history are directed and governed by Christ according to the Father's will for the sake of the church, his body.

We are given another reason for joy in the hope that Christ will establish and preserve his church by his word and Spirit. This is the church to which he has knit himself. To each of the living stones, eternally chosen and redeemed by his blood, Christ is joined by his Spirit. To himself Christ joins a body with infinite variety and diversity and makes us all one in himself. Against that church, which Christ builds upon himself, the solid rock, the gates of hell cannot prevail. We rejoice in the preserving grace of our Lord Jesus Christ that keeps us as living members of his church.

As members, then, of his church, as sheep of his flock, we rejoice because the Lord cares for us.

He does care for us, does he not? Is he not our shepherd, because of whose care we lack nothing? Is he not our great high priest, who knows our tribulations and constantly seeks from the Father and obtains for us the grace sufficient for each day? Is he not our refuge and rest in times of trouble? Has he not carried us through the fires and the floods of life? Has he not shown that he is ever-merciful and gracious? Rejoice that, because the Lord is your shepherd, you lack nothing.

Regarding those things that we need each day, rejoice in the sure promise that your God shall supply all your needs according to his riches in glory by Christ Jesus (Phil. 4:19).

Another reason for joy is the privilege that Christ has given us to serve him together in the fellowship of the saints. The Lord, having saved us, does not save us and preserve us like a fine heirloom, placed in a locked cabinet, there to be observed unmoved. The Lord, having saved us, gives us the privilege to be his servants in his holy temple. He has given us the privilege to spend ourselves for the cause of his kingdom and covenant. He has given us that privilege to work together in a congregation for the faithful proclamation of his gospel or to work to our utmost in the faithful education of our children. He has given us the privilege to witness, in our daily life and work, of the greatness of our Lord and of his grace.

Under the faithful proclamation of the word of Christ, you are given a great reason for joy. There, through the word preached, Christ is not silent to us. He does not leave the child of God to guess what he is thinking, or what he might be saying at God's right hand about him. Through the preaching of the word, Christ declares the love of the Father for his church. Therein he reveals his grace and goodness toward us; he declares our justification; and he assures us of eternal life. He works in us powerfully, by that means, a growing faithfulness and a life of thankfulness. Rejoice that the word of the Lord is powerful to save and powerful to comfort.

As we live at the end of the ages, there is also reason for joy in the fact that God has graciously preserved and entrusted to us the rich heritage of the Reformed faith. Rejoice in the truth of God's sovereign, particular, unconditional, and adorable grace in the Lord Jesus Christ!

Concerning all those promises of the Lord to bless us, be joyful! Those promises are not shaky, uncertain, man-dependent possibilities. God's promises are rock-solid in the Lord Jesus Christ for his people. Although they are proclaimed through all the earth unto countless generations, yet they, by the Spirit and grace of Christ, are fulfilled particularly in believers and their spiritual seed. Rejoice greatly when God in his grace fulfills his promises in your life.

Rejoice evermore, because the Lord will work all things together for good (Rom. 8:28). Rejoice that all the events in your life do not unfold arbitrarily and without any real purpose. Rejoice that the Lord sovereignly governs and fulfills every detail of your life, and does that with the goal of good. That goal is chiefly that, throughout your whole life, God's greatness and glory may be revealed. That goal is that you may fully taste and see that the Lord is good in the full salvation and glory that awaits us.

When ought we to exercise this fruit of joy? We must rejoice at many times in our lives.

We must rejoice in the Lord as we worship in God's house (Ps. 100:1–2) or worship God in family and personal devotions.

We rejoice when we may baptize our children and receive a token of God's covenant faithfulness.

We have great joy when we see our children walking in the truth (3 John 4).

We have joy when we see our children faithfully marry in the Lord.

We have an occasion to rejoice when God grants us, for another day, food and health, and grants that to us as a blessing for Jesus' sake.

Besides that, there are numerous other occasions and circumstances in which God provides us with ample reasons to grow in the gift of joy in him.

But now listen to God's word again in Philippians 4:4, where God through the apostle says, "Rejoice in the Lord alway: and again I say, Rejoice."

When ought we to exercise this fruit of joy? The Lord's answer is "alway." Rejoice, not only in times of spiritual positives in our lives, but also in times in which, according to our flesh, we would be prone never to do it.

Is it even possible to rejoice in the time of trouble and anguish?

How can a believer rejoice when he is persecuted for the name of Christ (Acts 5:41; Acts 16:25)? How can we glory in tribulations (Rom. 5:3)? How can the child of God rejoice when he is gripped in tribulations or in the dark way of depression or loneliness? How can we be joyful when afflicted with constant, gnawing pain? Joy when near the stepping stone of death and in the heat of that last battle (2 Tim. 4:8, 17–18)?

It is humanly impossible to bring forth this fruit of joy in such tribulations. Nevertheless, the Spirit of the Lord by his grace will have his own wonderful way with us, in us, and through us. After all, he is the master grower and pruner, working on and in us, who are his living branches and who are ingrafted into Christ. By his mighty word and grace he calls us in a living faith unto joy. He works in us by his grace the blessed fruit of joy, which is always *in him*.

Therefore, even in the darkest gloom and sadness, we possess in Christ that deep-seated, spiritual, heavenly, triumphant joy. Although when you and I might even feel physically or mentally miserable and lonely beyond description, yet by the grace of God we possess in the

Lord the joy that the misery of this life cannot destroy. We may still enjoy, even in the darkest gloom, that one and only constant delight: "That I with body and soul, both in life and death, am not my own, but belong unto my faithful Savior Jesus Christ."[1] And that is our one and only constant delight because Jehovah's almighty, tender, and sustaining mercy toward us endures forever (Ps. 90:14; Ps. 100:5).

May the Spirit of Christ guard us from all ungodliness that would pollute and quench this joy, and may he work in our regenerated hearts his wonder-fruit of heavenly joy—alway.

Questions for Discussion

1. Can a hypocrite have joy?

2. Is there a difference and a proper relationship between our spiritual joy and our emotional joy?

3. How can we rejoice in our good works without boasting and pride?

4. For what things in our daily life can we be joyful?

5. What affect will unconfessed sin and unholy anger in our lives have on our joy?

---

1 Heidelberg Catechism, A 1, in *The Confessions and the Church Order of the Protestant Reformed Churches* (Grandville, MI: Protestant Reformed Churches in America, 2005), 83.

Chapter 4

PEACE

Following love and joy, the next aspect of the fruit of the Spirit, according to Galatians 5:22, is peace. Like love and joy, peace is also a significant part of the believer's life. In fact, I believe that it would be fair to conclude that peace is very precious to you, dear reader. We would be most miserable without the peace that passes all understanding (Phil. 4:7) and without the blessed enjoyment of that peace with those in our earthly relationships.

True peace is not the illusive peace of the world. The illusiveness of the world's peace is seen among those nations and peoples who have been at war with each other for many years and whose attempts at peace have failed to yield reconciliation and an end to hostilities. The world will admit that in spite of its failures to broker lasting peace between warring nations and between warring groups in society, and in spite of civil unrest in many places, yet man can find a way out of his tangled mess of strife, hatred, envy, and war. Generally speaking, we hear the world proclaim that peace for man is what he can create on the foundation of his own wisdom, goodness, and righteousness. Man boasts that he can and will find solutions to his problems. He will build his kingdom of righteousness and peace in this earth.

Although the world boasts optimistically of an inevitable coming new world order of human peace, "there is no peace, saith the LORD, unto the wicked" (Isa. 48:22; Isa. 57:21). The reality is that the world of sinful and corrupt man is like the troubled waves of the sea: ceaselessly restless. That is true because man is by nature at war with God and refuses to confess that he is unrighteous and guilty. He willingly ignores that he stands under the condemnation and curse of God and is the recipient of God's wrath, which, even today at the end of the ages, he does reveal from heaven upon all ungodliness and unrighteousness of men (Rom. 1:18). Under that relentless firestorm and in the grip of that blasting typhoon of God's wrath, what real, lasting, unconquerable, and restful peace can man have?

The world has no true peace. One day it will have worldwide, earthly peace in the kingdom of the antichrist. Nevertheless, even while the world lives in tumultuous enmity against God, it remains under the billows and waves of God's fierce wrath, which will cast the unrighteous down to eternal destruction and endless, spiritual unrest. By nature that is where we would be too, except for the grace of God toward us in Christ Jesus. By nature we cannot have and cannot desire real peace.

By nature we are enemies of God and at war with him. Our sins are expressions of that spiritual violence and warfare against God's sovereignty and authority. By nature we do not want peace with God, but war with him in order to destroy him, if that were possible. Our daily sins testify of that spiritual enmity and war against God and our neighbor. Certainly, you and I may not have murdered anyone in a dimly lit, back alley, under the cover of a dark and rainy night. Nevertheless, we have slain our thousands, and our hands, unless washed clean by the blood of Christ, would be permanently stained with the blood of thousands, slain by our biting words, cruel gestures, envious thoughts, and murderous actions. For all our bullying, hostile confrontation, bitter envying, and all that is symptomatic of our enmity and warfare against God, we deserve not peace, but endless unrest under his curse.

Since true peace does not have its source in us, but in Christ alone, we rejoice that unto us, who are of ourselves unable to have, desire, and enjoy peace, Christ proclaims the wonder of his peace for us and in us. Unto his beloved church he proclaims, "Peace I leave with you, my peace I give unto you" (John 14:27). Jesus does have the authority and power to say this and to give unto his church peace because he is the Prince of Peace (Isa. 9:6). He has established this peace, and he gives this peace unto his eternally chosen church by his Holy Spirit.

What is this peace? This peace is fundamentally the peace of being right with God. We know that if one is not right with God, he stands before God under condemnation on account of his unrighteousness and guilt before the law. However, one who is right with God stands before God under no condemnation. He who is right with God is justified before God. He is justified before God not because of his own righteousness, for he has none, but because of the righteousness of the Lord Jesus Christ that God imputes to us through faith alone. Because we are justified by God, we stand in a relationship before God in which he is not at war with us, and we are not at war with him. Instead of the war that we deserve, there is for us only peace with God. That peace is the blessed fruit of our justification (Rom. 5:1).

The dearest part of this knowledge of our peace with God and, at the same time, the part that surpasses our understanding is that although our sins testify that by nature we were enemies of God, yet God is not at war with us. Though our sins are more than we can count, and the guilt of those sins piles up to an altitude beyond the height of Mount Everest or its neighboring lofty peaks, God justifies us through redemption in Christ Jesus. God declares us righteous and innocent in his sight on the basis of the obedience of Christ. He makes us partake of that blessing through faith alone. He views us as those who were never at war with him but who always delighted in peace with him. In turn, we learn through justifying faith that God is delighted in us and is not at war with us, but is at peace with us.

What is so amazing is that to establish this peace God made Christ to suffer the vengeance of his eternal wrath. What is amazing about this peace is that even while we were his enemies, Christ died for us (Rom. 5:10). While we were by nature so at war with God that we were guilty of the crucifixion of Christ, yet Christ so loved us that he died for us and reconciled us unto God by his atoning death. Therefore, God by the wonder of his grace has reconciled us unto himself in peace by the blood of the everlasting covenant (Heb. 13:20). In his covenant, God is at peace with us, holding us in the position of his favor always. Do you see now why peace is described in Philippians 4:7 as the peace that passes all your understanding?

True peace for us is that knowledge and assurance that all our sins are washed away in the blood of Christ and that God sees us not in our sin but in the righteousness of Christ alone. True peace for us is the knowledge and assurance that God is our heavenly Father who will always be at peace with us all the days of our life.

That peace is so dear to us because we have learned and continue to learn its great value in our present afflictions. Especially in times of afflictions that are sharp, sudden, deep, or drawn out, we are prone to wonder if God is at peace with us and whether we still are in the position of his favor.

We need to be reminded constantly by the truth set forth in Romans 5:1–5, which begins by declaring the great fruit of our justification by faith alone: peace with God! The passage continues to show that, being so justified and at peace with God, we stand in the position before God's throne of his favor and grace. Since we stand always before the face of God in that grace in peace with him, what then can our tribulations and afflictions be, except servants for our salvation and for our spiritual growth! For that reason, the apostle Paul could "glory in tribulations also" (Rom. 5:3). By faith he could do that because he knew that these things worked the blessed fruit of patience, experience, and an unashamed hope in the God who afflicts us for our eternal good and who, all the while, is at peace with us.

Or, there may be times in our lives when the guilt of past sins begins to trouble our souls.

We may endure sleepless nights, or nights with very little or restless sleep, because a troubled soul and mind are embroiled in the memory and stinging guilt of past sins. Precious is this peace when by faith we are led by the Spirit in the way of confession and an ardent looking to the perfect and complete atonement of Christ on his cross, offered not just for others, but also for us personally.

This knowledge of peace with God will appear to others as a spiritual calm in the midst of calamity. While our lives may be turned upside down outwardly, yet in this inner, spiritual peace with God, we receive whatever his hand gives us in life with contentment, patience, and trust. We trust that God, who looks upon us in his attitude of favor and who is at peace with us, does all things well.

Now, we do not always experience and live in this aspect of peace as we ought. We stand worthy of the rebuke of Jesus: "Why are ye so fearful? how is it that ye have no faith?" (Mark 4:40). The historical occasion for that rebuke was the disciples' lack of faith and trust in God and Jesus while they and Jesus crossed the Sea of Galilee in a gale that was for the disciples unprecedented. The ship was filling with water and Jesus was sleeping, and the disciples, being terrified, were quite certain that they and Jesus would perish. While they in reality had no reason to be fearful since the only begotten Son of God was with them, they doubted whether Christ really cared for them and would do anything to save them. In that unbelief, they had no peace, but only great fear.[1]

Are we really any different? In the face of catastrophe and crisis, quickly gone is the conscious knowledge and assurance of the truth that God always beholds us in his grace and has thoughts of peace toward us always for Christ's sake. Easily gone is the inner and unshakable confidence of peace that God will work out for good all and even our worst tribulations. How we need the Spirit of Christ to work in us that inner peace and rest in our souls, in which we know that Christ is for us, with us, and in us by his Spirit in the bond of his everlasting peace.

For the believer there is a refuge of rest and peace in the midst of this tumultuous life. There is a place in this life that is unconquerable from the violent waves of ungodliness that the world pours out in order to destroy the church. There is a place for the Christian soldier to go in the heat of the spiritual battles of this life against the violence of sin and ungodliness. There is

---

1 For an essay on how this incident in Jesus' earthly ministry, recorded in Mark 4:35–41, applies to our peace, see Don Doezema, "Peace," in *Jesus' Beauty Shining in You* (Grand Rapids, MI: Federation of Protestant Reformed Young People's Societies, 1989), 39–44.

a place near at hand, to which we may run in time of trouble and find restful refreshment for our souls.

That place of blissful refuge and unconquerable protection is under the shadow of the wings of the Almighty. In that place there is neither terror nor fear, but only that satisfying peace with God (Ps. 91:1–5). Let us enter that place in prayer and in worship to our heavenly Father faithfully and daily.

The outgrowth of this blessed peace with God is our peace with one another. Scripture shows that our enjoyment of peace with God affects our relationships with our spouses, children, fellow believers, and all whom God is pleased to bring upon our pathway. In fact, the enjoyment of peace in our earthly relationships is the perspective that Galatians 5:22 emphasizes when it speaks of peace along with the other aspects of the fruit of the Spirit.

One place in Scripture that describes the place of peace in the daily life of the believer is Colossians 3:15. There the Lord admonishes the redeemed and justified believer to "let the peace of God rule in your hearts, to the which also ye are called in one body."

There is only one true peace, and that is the peace of God. This peace cannot be found in the world and this peace the world will never have. The peace of God is the peace that Christ leaves with us and gives unto us by his Spirit on the basis of his perfect and complete atonement. This is the peace in which we know that we are right with God by faith alone and not by or because of our works. This is the peace that passes all understanding (Phil. 4:7) and for us is very precious. It is the prayer of the saints in Psalm 122 that this peace will flourish in the church. Sweet, spiritual harmony and unity in the doctrinal truth and the new life of our Lord Jesus Christ is the peace that we desire to be enjoyed among the brethren.

Now, how shall we enjoy that peace in this life? Just as we know the forgiveness of our sins by our heavenly Father in the way of our forgiving the sins of those who sin against us, so also we enjoy peace with God in the way of being a blessed peacemaker (Matt. 5:9), by doing those things "which make for peace" (Rom. 14:19), and by letting the peace of God rule in our hearts.

The kind of spiritual rule or government that we must desire for the peace of God in our life is illustrated by an umpire. "Rule" in Colossians 3:15 refers to the work and position of an umpire or a referee. We know that an umpire in a baseball game, a judge in a track and field event, or a referee in a hockey game determines whether the contestants compete fairly, applies the rules of conduct and fair play, and resolves any disputes between athletes or teams in order to maintain proper conduct and orderliness during the game or event. The umpire, judge, or referee ensures and promotes orderliness as the teams compete for the ultimate prize of the contest.

Unlike the goal of many ball teams and athletes today, the goal of the believer is peace in his relationship with his neighbor, especially in the home and in the church. His goal in life ought to be the enjoyment of the peace of God. Sometimes that goal is sought through spiritual warfare against spiritual enemies. Often it is pursued through the things that make for peace among the brethren. Whatever the situation may be, the ultimate goal is true peace.

At the very same time, that peace of God must be honored as the umpire or referee in our pursuit of peace. The peace of God ought to be enthroned as the referee to regulate and govern our consciences, thoughts, motives, reasons, decisions, speech, and attitudes. The peace of God is needed to remind us constantly that we must remain within the boundaries of love, longsuffering, gentleness, goodness, meekness, faithfulness, and self-control, which make for peace among the brethren. This is the peace that must be the umpire and must rule in our lives.

It is not the fruit of the Spirit that we allow the peace of man to be umpire, to which we are prone. In our sin, we do not want to turn the other cheek or to forgive seventy times seven.

We are prone to let the referees of revenge, retaliation, pride, selfishness, and love of earthly glory govern our hearts, minds, souls, and strength. Instead of the peace of God as umpire, we are prone to let be referee the sinful idea of making the one who sins against us to pay dearly for his offense and to suffer great misery because of it. When we are offended, we are prone to fight back in a sinful zeal for our own interests and pride. It is not difficult for us to examine our own lives and conduct and to find examples of our failures to let the peace of God rule and instead to allow sin and unbelief to enforce their rules.

When the peace of God rules in him, the believer lives and behaves in submission to the peace of God. When true peace is umpire, the believer does not retaliate in kind, but he follows the example of Christ, who did not retaliate when he was unjustly afflicted by wicked men (1 Pet. 2:23). When the peace of God rules in his life, the believer lives in the truth that God did not make war with us when we sinned against him. In fact, when we were guilty of war with Christ, he died for us in order to redeem us from our warfare against him and to unite us to himself in the bonds of love and peace.

This truth determines that our conduct toward those who sin against us ought to follow the truth of what God has done to us in Christ. Since God made peace with us through the blood of Christ, so in response to those who sin against us, we must make peace and reconciliation at the foot of the cross with brother, sister, spouse, child, fellow member in the church, and whatever neighbor the Lord may be pleased to bring upon our pathway.

As umpire, the peace of God ought to govern our attitudes toward those who do us good and toward those who do evil against us. When we remember the peace of God and submit to the truth that God made peace with us, our attitude toward those who do evil against us will become characterized by humility, love, and calmness. This fruit of the Spirit of peace is the opposite of a flaring, firecracker temper and a contentious, bullying spirit.

As a result, the peace of God as umpire will affect the manner of our conduct toward others. It guides us away from the extremes that are poisonous and toward those things that make for peace in the church and in the home. It guards us from conduct that is overzealous, like a rambunctious bull in an antique shop, and from conduct that is spiritually lazy, like a slow, slimy slug on a sidewalk. The peace of God guides us down the paths of wisdom and prudence in our lives with one another. When we step outside the boundaries of godly conduct, the spiritual referee of God's word functions as a mighty blast, like a shrill-sounding, heart-pricking referee's whistle! If necessary, we need the referee of peace to prick our hearts by the word and, if necessary, to chastise us with a firm rebuke.

The peace of God has as its ultimate goal the glory and honor of God. Peace may never be brokered at the expense of God's glory, honor, name, and truth. The true peace of God that shines forth with the truths of his sovereign, irresistible grace honors the name of God. And when that peace rules in our hearts, we are directed unto the same goal of God's glory and in the same way of faithfulness to the truth of our peace with God in Christ Jesus.

Now, where does the desire and obedience that the peace of God rules our relationships in life begin? This begins in the heart. The Spirit must work this remarkable and sweet fruit of peace in us. He must work not only the peace of the forgiveness of our sins, but also the peace of the forgiveness of those who sin against us.

For the growth and maintenance of that peace with one another, there is the gift of prayer. Faithful submission to the preaching of the word of the gospel develops and maintains this peace. In the way of thoughts that are true, honest, just, pure, lovely, and of good report, this peace is nurtured. Another chief way is living with one another in the way of confession of sin, forgiveness, and reconciliation in the blood of Jesus Christ. A life of contentment and humility serves the enjoyment of the gift of peace among brethren in the Lord.

Our daily experience shows that the maintenance of peace in the home and in the church is always accomplished through struggle. The Lord has it that way for us in this life so that we do not boast in ourselves and, instead, continually seek and trust him alone for the grace to live in this fruit of the Spirit.

In that regard, we may understand that the reason for the rule of peace in our hearts is that we are called into one body (Col. 3:15). We are not created and called by Christ into a body of disunity, but into his fellowship and life, which is one life. Since we are called into that one body of Christ and the life of that body is the peace and unity of Christ, it follows that we ought to pursue the expression of that unity in the home and in the church. We ought to desire even that unbelievers who are brought providentially upon our pathway be called out of the disunity and enmity of their sin and unbelief into the unity of repentance and faith in the Lord Jesus Christ alone. Furthermore, with that as the reason for our pursuit of true peace, we will seek the peace and prosperity of the church first. This may require that we deny ourselves, swallow our pride, and sacrifice our preferences, lest we injure and interrupt the peace of the home or the congregation. The blessed peacemaker will at the expense of himself let peace rule and reign.

When we consider how this fruit comes to visible expression in God's people now, it is evident that we depend upon the Spirit of Christ to produce this blessed fruit in us and to make the means of its growth effective in our hearts and lives. What a blessing it is when the Spirit by his grace gives us the opportunities to harvest and taste this fruit in our lives. The taste of peace and unity with the brethren is of great delight!

However, the difficulty of the enjoyment of this peace in this life is shown by examples in Scripture. For example, do you remember the sharp disagreement between the apostles Paul and Barnabas over the question of whether John Mark should be taken on the second missionary journey? Barnabas was determined to take John Mark. The apostle Paul determined that it would not be good to take John Mark because of his past departure from the missionary team on the earlier journey. The lines of disagreement were clear. The contention between the two was so sharp they were forced to part ways. There is no question in our minds about the orthodoxy either of Paul or of Barnabas. They were equally committed and faithful servants of Christ. Yet, in God's providence, for the peace and the good of the church, they parted ways according to the Lord's good pleasure (Acts 15:36–41).

I am quite sure that you can readily think of such situations in your own lives where for a time, due to struggle, sin, or controversy against false doctrine, the enjoyment of peace was affected adversely and even interrupted for a time.

Nevertheless, it is through such struggle and through reconciliation in the Lord, in faithfulness to the truth of God's word and to a life that follows from the truth of God's word, that by the grace of God the peace enjoyed afterwards becomes more precious and dear to those who truly desire in prayer and pursue in word and deed the peace of Zion here below.

You and I do take the blessed fruit of peace for granted all too often. We learn that fault especially when the Lord humbles us and withholds from us the enjoyment of his peace in times of testing, controversy, struggle, and our own sins. May we pray all the more earnestly that by the power of the blood of Christ and his Spirit peace may reign in our hearts and lives, and that we may delight to have Christ, our peace, so rule in and among us.

> How pleasant and how good it is
> When brethren in the Lord
> In one another's joy delight
> And dwell in sweet accord (*Psalter* 369:1).

Questions for Discussion

1. In what ways is the believer amazed at how God has given us peace with him?

2. How does this peace help the saint who may be suffering in afflictions?

3. Is it possible to enjoy peace with God while we are at war with fellow saints?

4. Give examples from church history in which the church was required to fight spiritual battles in order to maintain true peace with God in his truth.

5. In what ways can the enjoyment of peace be interrupted in our lives and cause misery?

Chapter 5

LONGSUFFERING

Longsuffering is first in the second main group of what is called, in Galatians 5:22, "the fruit of the Spirit." While the first group of three virtues (love, joy, and peace) seems to emphasize inner virtues, the second group of three virtues (longsuffering, gentleness, and goodness) seems to highlight virtues that are evident in our outward dealings and communication, especially with those of our church families and covenant homes.

Longsuffering begins the second set of aspects concerning the fruit of the Spirit because it is basic to gentleness and goodness. If one is not longsuffering, he will be harsh and unjust, rather than gentle; and he will be motivated by carnal and self-centered evil, rather than goodness. However, in the way of longsuffering, one is characterized by true gentleness and his actions will be governed by a spiritual and salvation-oriented goodness.

Longsuffering is a very honorable virtue. This aspect of the fruit of the Spirit was highly honored by the church father Chrysostom. He exercised it by the grace of God through unjust treatment and persecution. He spoke of it highly when, it is reported, he said that he regarded longsuffering as the queen of virtues. While love is the king of virtues among the nine virtues of the fruit of the Spirit, longsuffering certainly must be the queen.

According to this church father's example and testimony, we should desire and pray that the Lord by his Spirit and grace will give us the royal privilege to honor the queen of virtues by our conduct and speech with the members of our church families and covenantal families.

In Colossians 1:11, we are taught that we need both the gift of patience and the gift of longsuffering. The apostle Paul writes, "Strengthened with all might, according to his glorious power, unto all patience and longsuffering with joyfulness."

In our common daily conversation these words seem to be interchangeable, so that sometimes we talk about the need for patience with another person or our children; and yet it is possible that we might mean longsuffering. Although they may seem to be almost identical terms, according to Colossians 1:11 patience and longsuffering are shown to be both closely related and yet distinct virtues.

Patience may be described as the virtue of spiritual endurance through life. It is the spiritual strength to endure trials and afflictions in our God-given place and circumstances in life. Although there are many hardships that God bestows on his saints, the patience of the saints is the gift of God to receive those hardships willingly from the hand of God and to remain content in them.

Have you heard of the patience of Job?

Scripture calls us to consider the patience of that Old Testament saint. The patience of Job was his God-given spiritual endurance in the midst of the grievous hardships of the loss of his earthly possessions and his ten children in one day. In patience Job endured the affliction in faithfulness to God. This was evident when he acknowledged willingly in his grief that his sharp calamity came from the hand of his God (Job 19:21). While acknowledging that his calamity came from God, he confessed that God was good.

Listen to his patience: "Naked came I out of my mother's womb, and naked shall I return thither: the Lord gave, and the Lord hath taken away; blessed be the name of the Lord. In all this Job sinned not, nor charged God foolishly" (Job 1:21–22).

What a remarkable virtue to receive not only in times of great calamity, but also in the every-day challenges, hardships, troubles, and duty of daily cross-bearing.

Interestingly, the Bible does not use the word

patience with respect to God. The reason for this is that God does not suffer afflictions and calamities, as Job did or we do. Of course, Jesus did because he came into our flesh and was like us in all things, except for sin. Nevertheless, the Bible does not say that the triune God is patient. Patience is the spiritual virtue that our heavenly Father works in his saints so that they can sojourn faithfully in the pathway through which he is pleased to lead them. In the God-given gift of patience, we endure through the grievous pains and numbing griefs of this life, similar to our fellow saint Job.

In addition to patience for a faithful earthly sojourn, we need the gift of longsuffering. While patience is a virtue of the child of God with respect to his God-determined and providentially-governed circumstances in life, longsuffering is the virtue that applies to the persons whom God providentially places upon his divinely determined pathway and, as a result, with whom he cannot avoid communication and dealings.

The Bible does speak of God's longsuffering, in which he is longsuffering to all of his elect in Christ Jesus, not willing that any of the objects of his electing love should perish (2 Pet. 3:9). This is God's virtue whereby he, in his mercy and goodness, wills our eternal salvation and glory through the wilderness of this life. In his longsuffering, God wills our final perfection with him in glory; but before we reach that inheritance, we must be prepared for that glory in the best possible way. Tailored to each of us according to his good pleasure, our pathways include the suffering of afflictions, the suffering of temptations, and the suffering of the results of sin, corruption, unbelief, or weaknesses of others. In that way, God is pleased to demonstrate the power of his mercy to preserve us and to sustain us unto our glorious inheritance.

Colossians 1:11 reminds us that this attribute of God is reflected in his regenerated and sanctified people. That God's saints are longsuffering means that they bear with the weaknesses of others. Believing husbands and wives learn to be longsuffering toward each other. Brothers and sisters in the home learn to be longsuffering toward one another in order to prepare them for a life of longsuffering to others later in life. For peace in the home, parents and children learn to be longsuffering toward one another, especially so for children when bearing with the weaknesses of their parents, whom the Lord has set over them in authority. Fellow believers learn the necessity of longsuffering toward one another for the maintenance of the fragile peace and unity of their church family.

Being longsuffering, we will not retaliate in kind to those who sin against us, oppress us, or even inflict some obvious injustice upon us. The longsuffering that the saints demonstrate in their earthly life indeed reflects God's longsuffering toward us. Just as God does not in his justice destroy us and deal with us according to our iniquities, but, instead, deals with us according to his mercy and virtue of longsuffering, so we learn to deal with others not according to their sin, in order to reward them double for the pain they have inflicted upon us, but to deal with them according to the mercy of the Father shown toward us. Being longsuffering, we will be ready to forgive and to express that forgiveness to the sorrowful and repentant.

We may, then, describe the gift of longsuffering as that ability to be slow to anger and wrath. Longsuffering is wise on how to answer an offender. Longsuffering expresses itself as self-restraint, in which one does not break out toward an offender in an unrighteous and rash fit of rage. It keeps in check a flaming temper and controls the tongue from speaking evil. Longsuffering demonstrates its sweetness in forgiving seventy times seven.

To be longsuffering includes believing that God is judge, who judges righteously the hearts of others, which we cannot do. Longsuffering leaves in the Lord's hands judgment that belongs with him. We may want to take justice into our own hands, especially regarding the weaknesses and sins of someone over us in authority, and justify our rebellion against that sinful authority figure because of his or her sins and offenses, but such a response is still rebellion. We must be longsuffering even in such cases and leave in the Lord's hands the righteous judgment that he will dispense to those who walk in sin. We must also be confident that in his righteousness and mercy he will surely bring his people, also when they sin against us, to repentance.

The exercise of the virtue of longsuffering toward others does not include tolerance of the sin and unbelief of others. Longsuffering does not mean that we allow others to think that we approve of or will tolerate their false teachings or wicked way of life against God. Longsuffering remains holy as God is holy. Longsuffering does not ignore our duty to uphold courageously and outspokenly the honor and glory of God's name when his name is taken in vain. However, when our name and reputation are at stake, longsuffering is willing to suffer our reputation and name to be unjustly ruined.

There are two examples in Scripture of long-suffering worthy of consideration and instruction. First, in Numbers 12:3 we learn that the Lord regarded Moses, one of the holiest of God's saints, as the meekest man in the earth. The convergence of that holiness and meekness came to expression in his longsuffering toward his sister Miriam. In the event recorded in Numbers 12, she rebelled against Moses and instigated a serious insurrection against him, the God-appointed leader of the children of Israel through the wilderness. In longsuffering Moses let God judge Miriam's personal attack upon Moses. Then, when God did strike Miriam with leprosy, the righteous chastisement for her rebellion and schism, Moses did not rejoice in her leprosy and her great public shame. Instead, Moses cried unto Jehovah, saying, "Heal her now, O God, I beseech thee." And Miriam was healed—through the means of the significant longsuffering and earnest supplication of Moses.

Christ is the supreme example of longsuffering. When Christ "was reviled, [he] reviled not again; when he suffered, he threatened not; but committed himself to him that judgeth righteously" (1 Pet. 2:23). He endured suffering at the hands of sinners, including his own people, and submitted to his heavenly Father's way. He suffered long with his people who sinned against him. Although he was forsaken and denied by his disciples, he did not retaliate in kind. He did not deny his unfaithful disciples before his heavenly Father. He confessed their names before the throne of his heavenly Father in his longsuffering and prayer, saying, "Father, forgive them, for they know not what they do." What applied to his disciples applies to his church. Though we are sinners against him, he suffered long with us, even to his atoning and redeeming death of the cross for the purpose of our bearing forth this fruit of the Spirit, being ourselves longsuffering one toward another in the household of faith.

According to Colossians 1:11, longsuffering, in addition to patience, is a spiritual gift intended to be exercised by the believer in "all" things. Of course, it may seem rather easy to be longsuffering in most things with someone whom we like or when his personality fits very well with our own. When the weaknesses of another do not require much self-denial and the swallowing of our own pride and of our self-justification, we may find it very easy to suffer long with the fellow church member, spouse, parent, or child.

However, when longsuffering is applied in all things, then it applies even in those circumstances in life where we would judge that longsuffering no longer is the appropriate attribute to show the fellow church member, spouse, parent, or child whose weaknesses have found the end of our mercy and our willingness to forgive. In exactly those situations where we would conclude that it would be unfair of God to require us to be longsuffering, then also must we be longsuffering.

Hence in every circumstance and to our fellow believers, parents, spouses, and children, we must bear with their weaknesses and sins, even when those sins, from which they may have repented and been delivered by the grace of God, have caused serious and lasting scars.

Who can be longsuffering in all things or truly longsuffering at all? Christ certainly is. He is longsuffering as God to will our salvation through this wilderness of sin, death, and troubles. He is also the man who is longsuffering toward us in bearing long with us in his mercy and grace. He does not retaliate when we have sinned against him. He does not reward us double punishment for all our sins against him. He forgives our iniquities and has washed us in his blood from our sins. Even though our sins hurt as deeply as the great depths of suffering on the cross, yet he loved us and was longsuffering toward us. Likewise, by his Spirit, we are taught to be longsuffering toward fellow church members, spouses, parents, and children.

Undoubtedly, to be longsuffering requires the miracle work of the Spirit of mercy and truth in us. Only by and according to his glorious power and mercy can we bear long, longer, and longer yet, if necessary, with the weaknesses of others.

May we regard highly this sweet fruit of being longsuffering, and may we resolve in our hearts to be longsuffering in our daily lives, homes, and church life. There is no joy in despising or minimizing this fruit. In the way of evil speaking, harsh retaliation, jealousy, rebellion, hatred, and whatever else may be the enemy of longsuffering, there will be only bitter, rotten, and miserable results. Over against that, may our heavenly king, the Lord Jesus Christ, in his good and sovereign mercy, work in us the will, ability, and life of his queen of virtues.

Questions for Discussion

1. Do the words *patience* and *longsuffering* have the same meaning in the Bible?

2. How does learning as a child to be long-suffering to one's parents train a child for the fruit of longsuffering later in life?

3. May we say that Eli was longsuffering toward his wicked sons?

4. In what ways is God longsuffering to us?

5. What is the purpose of God's longsuffering toward us?

GENTLENESS

The next fruit of the Spirit in Galatians 5:22 is gentleness. This word is sometimes translated elsewhere in the Bible as "kindness."

This is another virtue that we learn to desire and that we pray that the Spirit of Christ will work in us more and more by the means of grace and his inner working. In fact, it is one virtue that the Lord calls us to put on: "Put on therefore, as the elect of God, holy and beloved,...kindness" (Col. 3:12). We must put on, or clothe ourselves with, gentleness toward one another in the household of faith.

What is gentleness or kindness?

Gentleness is a virtue of God himself. In Luke 6:35, we learn that our heavenly Father is "kind unto the unthankful and to the evil." In that verse Christ teaches us to be kind unto our neighbors upon the earth. The basis for that command of Christ is that the Father is kind unto the evil and unthankful. Certainly that is very true concerning the salvation of God's people. He is very gentle unto the unthankful and evil, such as we are. In fact, while we were yet his enemies, the Father sacrificed Christ for us and thereby redeemed us from our sin, evil, and unthankfulness toward him. That is the greatest demonstration of God's kindness unto his people, who in their sin and according to their nature are evil and unthankful. In spite of our evil and unthankfulness, the Father in his sovereign kindness saves us according to his eternal counsel. Now, according to that example and on that basis, we are called to reflect that gentleness unto our earthly neighbors in all our dealings with them.

That glorious kindness of the Father toward his elect in Christ Jesus arises out of his grace. We are taught that truth in Ephesians 2:7: "That in the ages to come he might shew the exceeding riches of his grace in his kindness toward us through Christ Jesus." Here we learn that the grace and goodness of God flow unto us through Christ Jesus in this way of kindness. Although we deserve a crushing and eternal blast of God's indignation because of our sin, yet God in his grace is kind unto us. He is not kind unto those who are not in Christ Jesus. The "us" of Ephesians 1 is not all men, but, according to verse 4, the "us" refers to God's elect. To all those who are not chosen by the Father, God is not kind, but righteously severe in his wrath and indignation. God handles the wicked, whom he curses, with a rod of iron. However, in contrast to the unrighteous, God is gentle and marvelously kind unto the righteous. Even though the people of God show that they are just as unthankful and evil sinners as the wicked, and sometimes even worse, yet God delivers them from their sin, heals them from their spiritual death of evil, blesses them with new life in Jesus Christ, and works in them the glory of eternal salvation. This is the wonder of God's sovereign, unmerited, and unconditional gentleness toward undeserving sinners. Have you experienced that gentleness of God?

We sing of his gentleness toward us:

Mindful of our human frailty
Is the God in Whom we trust,
He Whose years are everlasting,
He remembers we are dust (*Psalter* 281:1).

Thy free escape is my shield,
My sure defense in every strait;
Thy hand upholds me, lest I yield;
Thy gentleness hath made me great
(*Psalter* 35:6).

Jesus lived this virtue of kindness and gentleness toward his people in his earthly ministry. He was not gentle toward everyone in his ministry. Jesus pronounced judgments upon the cities, including Jerusalem, that rejected him and all the prophets that he sent to Israel. Those pronouncements of desolation, destruction, and woe were his word of harsh judgment on account of their pride, sin, and unbelief. Moreover, Jesus spoke very harsh and damning words to the unrighteous Pharisees, even calling them snakes and children of Satan. The gentle Lord will crush his enemies and deal with them in harshness.

However, unto his own he is neither harsh nor bitter. For example, when his disciples repeatedly did not understand his work as the Messiah, he did not lash out at them to destroy them and retaliate against them for their unbelief. He rebuked them in his love and grace. In kindness that seeks the salvation and true comfort of his elect sheep, Jesus called his disciples to repentance and true faith in him.

Jesus demonstrated his kindness powerfully to the woman who had been caught in the very act of adultery and was set in all her shame publicly before Jesus and a large crowd of people. The Pharisees were brutal and selfishly harsh with that woman. They had no compassion for this sinner and had no desire to give her any covering for her shame whatsoever. They abused that sinner for their own agenda of a public discrediting of Christ's work and person.

However, the good and kind shepherd controls his sheep. Unwittingly, the Pharisees were a tool in the hand of the Lord to bring the woman to the right place: her merciful savior. Christ in his mercy was kind unto her. As her merciful high priest, he said to her, "Neither do I condemn thee" (John 8:11). Forgiven! Jesus did not flatten this wicked sinner, who stood in the shame and the guilt of her terrible sin before the Lord. He did not crush the bruised reed, nor quench the smoking flax (Isa. 42:3). As her Lord, he forgave her sin.

Does that mean that in his kindness Jesus minimized the seriousness of the woman's adultery? No. Jesus could forgive her sin because he took that heinous iniquity upon himself and willingly was determined to suffer for this woman the crushing and bruising blow of God's wrath for her and all adulterers and fornicators like her, who are of his sheep. And in his kindness Jesus did not tolerate her sin. He spoke to her the kind and powerful word of life by which he called her out of her sin into the way of sexual purity and of thankfulness: "Go, and sin no more" (John 8:11).

Another example of this gentleness of Christ is how Jesus handled Peter when Peter was in the courtyard of the high priest's residence. After some time had passed since the last time that Peter yielded to the temptation to deny Jesus, Peter responded to a remark from another in the courtyard who affirmed that Peter was one of Jesus' disciples. Peter for the third time denied Christ. (Who of us would not have done the same thing?) After the echo of Peter's defiant denial and the crow of the courtyard rooster had almost faded, "the Lord turned, and looked upon Peter" (Luke 22:61). Jesus did not destroy Peter, nor did he yell angrily across the courtyard at Peter. Jesus looked right into the heart and soul of Peter, so that Peter remembered that Jesus foretold that Peter would deny Christ exactly as he had just done. Jesus brought Peter to repentance with that gentle but soul-piercing look of mercy.

Does not the Lord deal similarly with us in his kindness? Do you recognize that gentle, but soul-piercing look of your Lord to bring you to repentance and faith in him?

Think about how Jesus handled the little children of believers. Did he in cruelty send the parents and the little infants away as though he had no time for the lambs of his flock? Did Jesus tell the children that he has nothing to say to them but only to their parents? Did he tell the children that he has no blessing for them as infants and they must wait until they become adults? We learn that Jesus gathered his little lambs in his arms and blessed them with the blessings of salvation.

That same gentleness of our great shepherd toward his lambs is taught in Isaiah 40:11: "He shall feed his flock like a shepherd: he shall gather the lambs with his arm, and carry them in his bosom, and shall gently lead those that are with young." When we bring our children under the means of grace, including the preaching of the word and the sacrament of baptism for our infants, we behold the wonder of Christ's gentleness toward us and toward our seed to bless us and them with his undeserved and unmerited blessings of salvation.

"Who touched me?" Jesus said to a large crowd, including the woman who had touched the hem of his garment. She was timid and shy and thought she could obtain her healing unnoticed. But that is not the way Jesus works salvation. He brings us to stand before him face-to-face and to confess our salvation with heart and mouth before him, before his church, and even before the world. Jesus is our savior and covenant-friend, who joins us in close fellowship with him. Thus did Jesus bring before him the woman who touched his garment, so that she might unburden her soul. And in response, Jesus said, "Daughter, be of good comfort: thy faith hath made thee whole; go in peace" (Luke 8:48).

Similarly, Jesus deals with us, who are of a weak faith and are also often reluctant to cast all our care upon him. We must remember that he in his gentleness does care for us and remains near to us in his care through the Comforter, his Spirit.

Based on what gentleness means with respect to our heavenly Father and our Lord Jesus

Christ, we may then describe the gentleness of the elect, regenerated, and sanctified children of our heavenly Father.

True gentleness for us is the virtue that is the opposite of and is also opposed to all spiritual brutality, hostility, and harshness. Gentleness is not cruel. It is never motivated by a spirit of retaliation by which we decide that the offender must pay double for the pain that he or she has inflicted on us. Gentleness does not strike back. It is not proud. It will not hurtfully poke fun of the afflictions, disabilities, weaknesses, and acute problems of others.

Gentleness is a virtue by which the child of God, who is the covenant-friend of God, shows himself to be spiritually friendly to other members of the body of Christ. It is a virtue by which the child of God deals with fellow believers, not to crush them, but to build them up and to deliver them from spiritual ruin. It is a virtue that regards covenantal friendship and life in the body of Christ as very fragile and precious and a gift of God to be handled delicately. It is a virtue of the handling of the souls of others with great care. It is a virtue that parents must exercise toward their children, whereby the parents handle the souls of their children cautiously, without crushing them under the fist of a tyrant or under the impossible, Pharisaical burdens of endless rules. Instead, the lambs of Christ are handled with his gentleness, which guides the children by instruction and consistent discipline out of the way of sin and unbelief and into the way of faith and a thankful life. The goal of that gentleness is that the children grow up smiling in the fear and admonition of the Lord.

From whence comes this virtue of gentleness? Is it a natural ability that one can acquire by birth or by sufficient education? By nature we are cruel and harsh. True gentleness, gentleness that meets the standard of excellence of the Holy Spirit, cannot have its origin in us. In fact, a man might be naturally and sincerely gentle toward another miserable and hurting individual while at the same time tolerating that other person's sin and not speaking as Christ did to the woman caught in adultery. A woman may handle her child with great gentleness and raise that child in a gentle spirit that might make the leaders of Hinduism, Buddha, or Islam proud. A man or woman's natural gentleness or sincere gentleness in bondage to a false religion does not meet the Holy Spirit's standards of quality and excellence for his fruit.

All that is of man is spiritual enmity and bitterness against God and against one another. Where enmity and sin rule in the heart of a man, no true gentleness will result. In fact, where enmity rules in a man's heart, that becomes evident inevitably in his words and actions toward God and especially toward one another. For example, if a husband or a wife lives in the sin of bitterness and harshness toward the other, then his or her thoughts, words, and actions of harshness and brutality will crush, hurt, and suffocate the life and beauty of what the marriage bond ought to be in view of the gentle Christ toward his beloved bride, the church.

The gentleness that meets the Holy Spirit's standard of excellence has its source in the love of Christ. The foundation and life-source of being kind to one another with a view to Christ and our heavenly Father is the love by which Christ loved us first and, as a result, the love whereby we love Christ first above all else. With that love of Christ in our hearts, there will be the beginning of a life of true gentleness. Where there is that self-denying, thankful, faithful love of Christ and unto Christ, there will be gentleness toward one another.

That love of Christ sees the great gentleness with which Christ has made beautiful and glorious his undeserving bride, his church. In thankfulness for that wondrous, gentle Lord and savior, there will be present in our hearts by the grace and Spirit of Christ the beginning of that gentleness toward our neighbor, especially toward those whom we know and love in our Lord.

Therefore, clothe yourselves with his gentleness, which is the command of the Lord in

Colossians 3:12: "Put on therefore, as the elect of God, holy and beloved, bowels of mercies, kindness." We must clothe ourselves with this virtue of kindness, or, as it is also called in Scripture, gentleness.

What is this spiritual fabric that must be worn by the regenerated, believing, holy child of God? It is certainly not clothing that we can fabricate. We can neither fabricate the clothing necessary to cover the shame and nakedness of our sin in the sight of God, nor manufacture this holy clothing of gentleness. This is a robe that God has made with the living and golden threads of the holy life of Jesus Christ. For us to wear this robe, the Spirit of Christ must put it on us through his word. He must give us the strength to wear it and to exercise this robe of gentleness in our daily life.

For that robe and the faithful wearing of it, we must pray unto our heavenly Father daily. We must seek the Father for the Spirit and grace to wear it and to exercise it.

To whom, then, must we exercise this virtue of gentleness? We must be kind and gentle toward our fellow saints within the household of faith, the church. To those in the grip of grief and sorrow, to those walking in sin, to our covenant children, to our spouses, and to all whom the Lord in his providence brings upon our pathway in the life of the church, we must be kind.

Little children must learn to be kind and

gentle. At a very early age, we show by our fighting or by our theft of toys from the unsuspecting sibling that we are prone to be brutal, cruel, and hostile toward others. Instead, we must be kind to one another. We must be gentle toward others who may have disabilities, be wheelchair bound, or cannot learn and memorize as quickly as others. Diversity in the body of Christ is the God-given circumstance in which to exercise kindness.

In addition to that, we must even be kind to our enemies. The Scripture teaches us to give to an enemy a cup of cold water when he is thirsty (Rom. 12:20) and to be kind even to the unthankful and evil (Luke 6:35–36). Even in persecution, the believer must be gentle, as Christ was: "Who, when he was reviled, reviled not again; when he suffered, he threatened not; but committed himself to him that judgeth righteously" (1 Pet. 2:23).

When we consider the wide range of types of people to whom we must show kindness, that brings to mind some important characteristics of this amazing virtue of gentleness.

First, true kindness toward others ought to be unconditional. Just as we did not merit God's gentleness and compassion upon us, neither must we expect others to merit it from us. Freely must we put on and exercise this virtue of kindness. We must not wait for others to fulfill certain conditions and maintain a level of merit before we exercise gentleness. We must not wait for others to show gentleness to us before we will be gentle to them. God did not require us to fulfill conditions of gentleness first in order then to be kind to us. God loved us first (1 John 4:19). Even when we were his enemies, God in our savior was merciful and gentle toward us unto our redemption. Similarly, we must not exercise gentleness toward another on the basis of a set of fulfilled conditions and prerequisites. We must exercise unconditional and free gentleness toward others.

It should be clear, then, that kindness should be exercised to the undeserving. There are those who by their behavior make it extremely difficult for us to exercise kindness. In fact, to those who provoke us by their sins, we are prone to retaliate in kind, but never in kindness. Nevertheless, even to the unthankful and evil, we must be kind. Our kindness toward our children, for example, may not be based upon whether they deserve it or not. It is a fact that no man, woman, or child will ever be worthy of any kindness. Yet, Scripture requires us to exercise kindness even to evil and unthankful men, women, and children, who in their unthankfulness show themselves to be the most undeserving.

Next, true kindness is constant. God is eternally kind to us. Ought not we, as the children of our heavenly Father, be exercising this virtue constantly? Should we not be fighting diligently against retaliation, cruelty, bitter harshness, and spiritual brutality to others? Should we not be seeking by faith in Christ alone to put on that virtue of gentleness in word and action?

Let us not forget, though, that true kindness is also holy and righteous. We must not think that gentleness is never calling another to repentance. We must not think that a spiritually gentle father would never discipline his children. We must not think that gentleness avoids contending for the faith and doing the hard work of saying sharp words to a stubbornly impenitent sinner. True gentleness does not approve or tolerate sin. This is also illustrated by Christ in John 8:3–11. Jesus forgave the woman caught in the guilt and public shame due to her sin of her adultery. Jesus would not condemn her, but forgave her, because he intended to redeem her as well. However, Jesus did not say to her that it was permissible to continue in her sins against the seventh commandment. Instead, Jesus in his kindness called her out of her past ways of sin by saying, "Go, and sin no more!" Christ's kindness was both righteous in his forgiveness and holy in his call to forsake the ways of wickedness.

Such is the virtue with which we desire to be clothed upon by the Spirit of Christ. Our kindness may not tolerate sin, but must hate sin. In true kindness, we must call unrepentant sinners out of their sins of wickedness, or even of radicalism, into the holy and wise ways of repentance and faith in Christ. To those who confess their sins, kindness is righteously forgiving on the basis of the atoning sacrifice of Jesus Christ, and kindness will in holiness lead a repentant sinner out of his sin and into the holy and wise ways of the Father. In that way, true kindness honors our heavenly Father, is consistent with his love for us in Christ Jesus, and thereby shows that we are the children of our heavenly Father renewed by the Spirit in the image of Christ.

Finally, true kindness is filled with and governed by the word of God. It follows studiously the examples of the saints in Scripture. It is filled with the words and wisdom of Scripture for comfort, admonition, correction, and instruction in the paths righteousness.

In order that we might bring forth this fruit, the Lord calls or commands us by his word and Spirit: "Clothe yourselves with this kindness one toward another."

That command to do so is based upon the truth that we are the "elect of God" (Col. 3:12). This echoes the truth of election as taught in Ephesians 1:4. God has chosen us in Christ to be ordained unto eternal salvation through the wonder of our deliverance from sin by his grace alone. God has made this decree of election "before the foundation of the world." He has chosen us unconditionally and sovereignly unto salvation. According to God's will, Christ calls us the elect of God. We have been predestinated in Christ to be the sons and daughters of our heavenly Father in everlasting life with him.

The goal of that election, according to Ephesians 1:4, is holiness and blamelessness before him in the bond of love. The goal of that election is that we might be transformed into the image and life of Christ. We shall be like Christ in his glory, which includes all the virtues of that new man in Christ, including kindness. While we bring forth kindness in fulfillment of God's will and counsel, we know that we are the elect of God.

This finds support in what the apostle Paul taught in 2 Thessalonians 2:13: "God hath from the beginning chosen you to salvation through sanctification of the Spirit and belief of the truth." This teaches us that we are chosen unto that life of sanctification of the Spirit. We are chosen unto that life of bearing the fruit of the Spirit. In fulfillment of that will of God and eternal good pleasure of God in our salvation, Christ commands us to clothe ourselves not only with the new man in Christ, but specifically with kindness over against the cruelty, retaliation, bitterness, and harshness of our old nature.

Second, the command to clothe ourselves in kindness is based on our being called "holy" (Col. 3:12). It may be a surprise to us, at first, that God would even dare to call us holy. In response to our surprise, let us remember, first, that Christ is holy. He is pure in all his glory and being. He is totally consecrated unto the eternal good pleasure, the will, and the purpose of God. So holy was Christ that he could not yield to the sinful temptations from the devil. And now at God's right hand, Christ is beyond and above sin and temptation in his glory. He is holy, as God is holy.

By mentioning that we are holy, the apostle Paul reminds us that this is our new identity as members of the body of Christ, purchased by Christ, and now anointed and sanctified by his Spirit. In Christ we are holy. That is quite a statement in light of all our present wickedness and sin. Yet, that is true: belonging to Christ we possess now, in him, his holiness. Even though we possess only a small beginning of the life of that holiness, yet we are holy in Christ. This we confess in the Apostles' Creed when we say that the church is not only catholic, but also holy. We learn, of course, that the church is holy not because of her members, but only because of, and in, Christ by his sanctifying Spirit of holiness.

On the basis of that principle, Christ through his apostle declares that since we are holy, part of that life of holiness includes wearing the robes of gentleness one toward another. Live in consecration to your head, Jesus Christ, and desire to exercise this Christ-like virtue. Show that thankful love and heartfelt devotion to him in how you treat those who are also united to him and to you by his Spirit through faith.

Finally, the believer ought to clothe himself by faith with kindness because the child of God is called "beloved." The love of Christ for us and in us surpasses our comprehension of the dimensions and greatness of his love toward us. He so loved us first that he gave himself entirely to the atoning death of our salvation. He did that even though we did not deserve it and never will deserve his redeeming love. Still, Christ loves us with his constant, never failing love. Although we sin against him and his people, he does not destroy us. When we experience coming to our heavenly Father in repentance and prayer by the gentle and rescuing mercy of Christ, we also experience that Christ is at the throne of grace, not as our accuser or adversary, but as our gentle and kind advocate who pleads with the Father, on the basis of his merits alone, for the grace and mercy that we need moment by moment. That faithful and powerful love of Christ and his faithful supply of the grace and mercy that we need provide us the constant motivation to wear the virtue of kindness toward one another. That we are the beloved assures us that Christ has poured into us his love. He not only loves us by doing various things for us, but also his love carries through to the point where he fills us with his love by his Spirit. He unites us to himself in love, in the bond of perfection. Because he gave us his love, his life, and his Spirit, we have the possibility and the reality of a life of love toward him and of a life of the production of the fruit of the Spirit, including kindness.

That reminds us that without the exercise of love, the first aspect of the fruit of the Spirit, there will be no fruit of kindness. We have the hope that with the love of Christ by his Spirit in us his beloved, there will also come forth fruits of gentleness and kindness.

This faithful exercise of gentleness will result in peace. This is not the same as earthly peace or the end of all controversy and struggle. We may not expect that by the exercise of this virtue suddenly our pathway will become smooth, flat, and free of troubles or that it will be much different than it was for Christ in his earthly sojourn. Christ said that as we live like him the world will hate us because it hated him. Though we must exercise acts of kindness, yet do not expect that your lot in the midst of the world will improve because of this faithfulness to Christ. The world hates Christ. As the wicked and unbelieving behold in you the image of Christ, being more and more renewed daily by the work of the Spirit in the way of repentance and trust in Christ, they will despise the spiritual sweetness of your kindness. If not taking advantage of your kindness, the world will persecute you. The result of your spiritual gentleness, which does not compromise for sin and false doctrine, will be cruelty of various sorts from the proud and unbelieving.

Nevertheless, clothing ourselves with the virtue of kindness will have the result of the enjoyment of peace toward our heavenly Father as we seek to be as he is toward us. In that way, we will enjoy the priceless assurance that we are the Father's children. Furthermore, this exercise of gentleness will bear good fruit in our families and in our church homes. Where we exercise kindness one toward another, strife and schism stop and healing and the enjoyment of blessed peace begin. Where there is that peace, there is the enjoyment of having our gentle savior, by his word and Spirit, dwell within and among us.

Consequently, the result of kindness is an occasion for thankfulness. The end of our salvation is that God might be praised and thanked. Our gentleness is blessed by God with the result of thankfulness, sometimes immediately, and at other times over a long period of time, in those to whom we deal in a kind and gentle spirit.

Give thanks to God that he makes it possible by the wonder of his grace that we who were once dead branches are now living branches in Christ Jesus, to bring forth the fruit of gentleness. Believing in the gentleness of his sovereign and irresistible mercy toward us, let us, then, in thankfulness clothe ourselves with kindness toward one another.

Questions for Discussion

1. In what ways has God shown his gentleness to you?

2. How should friends, parents, and spouses demonstrate the fruit of kindness?

3. Give examples from the Bible of saints who showed the virtue of gentleness.

4. In what ways does the world's culture of sports often contradict the virtue of kindness?

5. What will be the results of the exercise of kindness in the family, in the church family, and even in our employment?

6. Why must we be kind to others?

Chapter 7

GOODNESS

So far, we have considered the truth that the fruit of the Spirit is love, joy, peace, longsuffering, and gentleness. Now, we consider that the fruit of the Spirit includes the virtue of goodness.

With the consideration of goodness, we once again can appreciate that the various aspects of the fruit of the Spirit are a blessed unity. For example, where there is the true love of Christ in us, there will also be present the virtue of goodness. One who truly loves his neighbor will also do good to him. Moreover, when one possesses the virtue of gentleness, he will express that gentleness to his neighbor by doing good to his neighbor. Goodness is an honorable virtue that we desire the Holy Spirit to work in and through us by his grace so that we can reflect our heavenly Father, who is "abundant in goodness" (Ex. 34:6).

What is the meaning of goodness? According to Scripture, the term seems to have two basic ideas. First, goodness sometimes refers to moral purity. According to Psalm 112:5, a good man is one who shows favor. He is also, according to the earlier verses, one who is filled with grace and compassion and who is righteous. Although he is a sinner, he lives daily in repentance and by faith in the way of gratitude to God for salvation. He fights his old nature manfully and finds deliverance in the power of the Holy Spirit. Such a man is upright in his heart (Ps. 125:4) and one who finds favor from Jehovah (Gen. 6:8; Prov. 12:2). In his godliness, he deals with others in righteousness and compassion. By this description of a good man, we understand that goodness is the spiritual health and wholesomeness of the sanctified and godly believer.

Second, goodness may emphasize the motive and purpose of someone's honorable thoughts and actions toward another. In that case goodness describes the purpose of the believer's actions toward another as heavenly oriented and God-centered. That goodness may have the viewpoint of purpose, or goal, is based on the use of "good" in Genesis 1. Soon after the creation of Eve, "God saw every thing that he had made, and, behold, it was very good" (Gen. 1:31). God meant by "good" not only that his creation originally possessed the virtue of life, order, and righteousness unto his glory, but also that the creation in its design and life was ready to be governed by God to his ordained purpose in Christ (Col. 1:15–20). The creation of all things for the purpose of Christ is good because that in the end will glorify Jehovah, our covenant God in Christ Jesus.

We believe that the goodness of the child of God by the sanctifying power of the Holy Spirit is the ability to do to others morally pure acts—that is, acts that have a proper and honorable purpose with respect to our Father in heaven and with respect to the person to whom we perform some particular act of goodness, such as giving food or words of encouragement to a fellow saint.

Since we are called to be imitators of our heavenly Father (Eph. 5:1) even with respect to this virtue of goodness, it is proper that we remember that Jehovah is good (Ps. 25:8). We are admonished to praise Jehovah for his goodness, which he bestows upon his people. "O give thanks unto the Lord, for he is good: for his mercy endureth forever" (Ps. 107:1). Later in that Psalm we are again commanded to praise God for his goodness (vv. 8, 15, 21, 31). God shows that he is good in his mercy toward his people, a mercy that raises them out of their misery unto the goal of their salvation and blessedness. Although the word "goodness" in these verses in Psalm 107 refers in the original Hebrew to God's mercy and lovingkindness, yet perhaps the Bible translators used "goodness" to reflect the close relationship between God's

mercy and his goodness toward his people.
God's mercy for his elect always works toward
the goal of our eternal happiness and peace in
Christ Jesus. For that reason we do and must
give Jehovah many thanks for his goodness
to us miserable sinners. God displays his
goodness when in his wrath and for the goal
of his own glory he destroys the wicked world
whom he hates. Indeed, God is truly good to his
church when in his mercy he saves his people
out of their sin and misery into the blessedness
and life of covenantal fellowship with him in
heavenly glory.

We confess this goodness of God when we
confess that our God works all things together
for good (Rom. 8:28). By this we confess that
God works all things together for his own glory
as our Father and for our inheritance of eternal
glory with him in the new creation. Every detail
of our life is designed and governed for that
glorious purpose, so that our life experiences
do not come to pass by luck, chance, or fate.
As a result of God's goodness to us, even our
light affliction in this present life works for us
that sure goal of the far greater weight of glory
with him.

It is unto that goal that God continues to be
good to us even though we often are not good
to him and come far short of the glory that we
owe him. Daily God shows that his goodness
is unconditional, undeserved, unmerited, and

unchangeable toward us in Christ Jesus. God is good, even to us who often behave so unthankfully and wickedly and who by nature are evil and unthankful. God remains good to his elect and works all things together for their good.

This goodness of God is revealed to us clearly in Christ. Jesus is our shepherd, full of the virtue of goodness. "I am the good shepherd," Jesus says to us and to our children (John 10:14). Indeed, his goodness is evident throughout all of his work and all of his treatment of his sheep and lambs. Psalm 23 illustrates to us several examples of the spiritual care that our good shepherd exercises over us all the days of our lives. He makes us to lie down in green pastures. He leads us beside still waters. He restores our soul with his refreshment and rest. He leads us in the paths of righteousness by going with us. He walks with us through the valley of the shadow of death, so that even there he does not forsake us. He protects us. He keeps us from straying off the path to our complete ruin. He leads us to plateaus above the dark valleys. He cares for us to ward off perilous sickness. He gives us an overabundant supply of all that we need. He is the good shepherd toward us because he is faithful, merciful, and committed to the goal of gathering and leading his sheep and lambs to his heavenly fold.

So committed is Christ to that goal, and so committed is he in his love to us and the

Father, that he laid down his life for us, and then took it up again as the Father gave him commandment (John 10:14–18). By that death and resurrection of Christ, we and the other sheep and lambs that yet remain to be gathered shall obtain their place in his heavenly fold. So sure is that goal that no man can pluck any of his sheep and lambs out of his hand of grace. So faithful is Christ unto that goal that, though we stray foolishly into sin, he will rescue us in his sovereign mercy (Luke 15:1–7). He is so good to us that he will always seek our everlasting good, so that we may dwell in the house of Jehovah forever.

Do you experience the goodness of Jehovah and of Jesus Christ to you?

We must display that goodness toward others and so imitate our heavenly Father and our Lord Jesus Christ. We must do that because we are living branches, united to the root and tree, Jesus Christ. Because the Holy Spirit has united us to Christ and made us one with the true vine, our goal and purpose is to bear fruit unto the glory of God (John 15:1–8). The purpose of our life in Christ is to bring forth the virtue of his goodness. And in the performance of that good we may be assured and see that we are the children of God (3 John 1:11).

The exercise of goodness involves the desire for the everlasting happiness of others. Of course, we desire the earthly happiness of others. We do not rejoice when a child, parent, relative, or fellow member in the church suffers from sickness or a disease that will lead them over the threshold of death. We desire the earthly health and prosperity of others. However, never may that desire for their earthly happiness interfere or contradict our desire for the goal of their spiritual health and spiritual happiness in Christ Jesus.

Certainly, the goal of our earthly assistance of others must be truly good. It must seek the glory of God and the salvation of others. When we assist fellow believers in the church in times of earthly need, our goal must be their spiritual encouragement. When the wicked neighbor endures a crisis in his life and we are there to help, our energetic assistance must seek the goal of an opportunity to witness of Christ and to seek the ultimate goal of his conversion, the Lord willing.

The exercise of goodness may mean that we must rebuke those who walk wickedly in sin. Such work with an erring church brother, family member, or a wicked neighbor in the neighborhood is not pleasant or easy. Nevertheless, with our heart full of the knowledge of what God has in his goodness done to us (turning us from our sin and setting us by his grace upon the way that leads to everlasting life), surely we will speak the necessary words to rescue, if possible, the erring brother or wicked neighbor from his sinful path down the broad and perilous way that leads to everlasting death.

The exercise of goodness reminds us of what is good for us. Christ is the good shepherd because he denied himself. Even when we were his enemies, he sacrificed himself for us, the goal of which is our salvation. That self-sacrifice is also good for us; it is good that you deny yourself, take up your cross, and follow Christ, for the good of your soul. It is good that we deny our own will and seek the will of our heavenly Father, whether in childhood, teenage years, single life, married life, or widowhood. It is good that we do outward good to others, even those who may seem the least deserving of any assistance and who may be our spiritual enemies, with the goal that they might be blessed and be led in the paths of righteousness for Christ's sake, the Lord willing.

Even our speech must be seasoned with goodness. Our speech and conversation with others must serve the purpose of spiritual edification. "Let no corrupt communication proceed out of your mouth, but that which is good to the use of edifying, that it may minister grace unto the hearers" (Eph. 4:29). Lest we fall into another extreme, the Lord admonishes us to speak the truth and to speak that truth in love. "But speaking the truth in love, may grow up in him in all things, which is the head, even Christ" (v. 15). When our speech and conduct are salted with goodness, we avoid the evils of wicked communication and of the radicalism of an unedifying and damaging communication of truth.

This virtue of goodness is very honorable and desirable. It is a spiritual beauty that the godly wife must covet because it characterizes the virtuous woman: "The heart of her husband doth safely trust in her, so that he shall have no need of spoil. She will do him good and not evil all the days of her life" (Prov. 31:11–12).

One who seeks to enjoy the secret of a truly happy life must covet this virtue of goodness. "For he that will love life, and see good days...let him eschew evil, and do good" (1 Pet. 3:10–11).

One who must admonish an erring brother needs to be equipped by God with goodness, without which proper rebuke is impossible. The apostle Paul wrote to the Roman Christians, "And I myself also am persuaded of you, my brethren, that ye also are full of goodness, filled with all knowledge, able also to admonish one another" (Rom. 15:14).

Who were the kings of Judah that were highly honored and fondly remembered by the people of God? They were the good kings, such as Hezekiah and Josiah. These two in particular were noted for their goodness toward the kingdom of Judah. We read, "Now the rest of the acts of Josiah, and his goodness, according to that which was written in the law of the Lord,

And his deeds, first and last, behold they are written in the book of the kings of Israel and Judah" (2 Chron. 35:26–27). Both Josiah and Hezekiah led Judah by their work of reformation from the wicked ways of sin and idolatry into the godly ways and fear of Jehovah. Their work had both an honorable, moral quality to it and that good purpose of the proper worship and life of the faithful service of Jehovah.

For what would you like to be remembered? Your sports trophies? Your hobbies? Your skills? The money and possessions you have acquired and can pass on to your children?

Should we not desire to be remembered for the virtue of goodness that shined clearly and brightly in our lives and labors through our actions to others unto the glory of God? Should we not desire to be remembered as those who did good to others, even to our enemies, with the good desire that they might fully enjoy the truth of our only comfort in life and death in Jesus Christ alone according to the standards of the Reformed faith?

Perhaps at some time in your life you have known a fellow saint who was gentle and truly good to you in a memorable way. If we are truly humbled before God, then what impresses us about such people is that their acts were done unselfishly to us, the least deserving, for the goal of our spiritual and eternal good. Why did they do such things to us? The answer is that the Lord works in his children that beauty and sweetness of goodness toward one another for his own glory.

For us and for those saints whom we remember as good, doing good is never easy in this life because of our ever-present sin and selfishness. Nevertheless, by the miraculous grace of the Holy Spirit, what blessedness it is when we bring forth the fruit of goodness to the glory of God and enjoy its sweetness in the communion of the saints.

May our Lord mercifully and powerfully continue to call us unto the practice of this virtue of goodness.

Questions for Discussion

1. How does the great shepherd demonstrate his goodness to you in your life?

2. Give examples from the Bible of God's goodness to his people.

3. Why is goodness a key virtue for proper admonition of others who may be sinning?

4. For what would you like to be remembered by others?

5. In what ways will this fruit of goodness affect our communication and speech to others?

Chapter 8

FAITHFULNESS

It is important to understand what we are examining here in the seventh part of the fruit of the Spirit. The seventh part of the fruit of the Spirit in Galatians 5:22 is faith. We may be inclined to think that this means saving faith, which, according to Lord's Day 7 of the Heidelberg Catechism, is the spiritual bond by which we are joined by God to Christ, the conscious activity of believing, and the catholic, apostolic, undoubted Christian truth of Scripture that is necessary for every Christian to believe.

However, that is not exactly what the word "faith" in Galatians 5:22 means as a fruit of the Spirit. There is no denying that the bond of faith, the activity of believing, and the doctrines of the faith are essential to and very involved with this virtue of faith in the fruit of the Spirit. In fact, one cannot separate the blessing of saving faith and the virtue of faith as a part of the fruit of the Spirit. Nevertheless, so that it is clear in our minds what we are discussing here, it is better to understand that the virtue of faith in Galatians 5:22 means "faithfulness."

Faithfulness is a spiritual virtue of the saint by which he is loyal toward the Father and Christ with the result that the saint is also loyal, reliable, and dependable toward others whom the Father providentially brings upon his pathway in life and whom he must serve in some way in his place and calling in life. When one is faithful to the Father and Jesus Christ as revealed in his word, he will be a faithful, trustworthy, and reliable Christian, member of his church, officebearer, spouse, friend, employer, employee, parent, school teacher, student, or child.

We see this virtue of faithfulness in all its perfection in Christ. In all of his labors Christ was faithful to the Father. Although Jesus did not call himself faithful in John 17:4, yet what he says reflects that he is the faithful servant of Jehovah. Jesus said, "I have glorified thee on earth: I have finished the work which thou gavest me to do." Implied in that statement is the faithful obedience of Christ in all of his labors in spite of the constant temptations of his adversary, the devil, and his enemies to forsake the way of obedience to his Father. When the hour of his work of redemption, by his atoning death on the cross, had come, Jesus was indeed faithful. He had never disobeyed his Father. He had always done the Father's will, not his own will. He maintained a voracious appetite for the Father's commandments for his life and work so that he could say to his disciples, "My meat is to do the will of him that sent me, and to finish his work" (John 4:34).

Of course, Jesus' faithfulness is clearly revealed at the cross. He loved his own to the very end. He laid down his life for them without complaint. He descended into the depths of hell for them on the cross without retaliation against them. The clear revelation of his faithfulness in his own mind was heard in the confident cry of Jesus, "Father, into thy hands I commend my Spirit." Had Jesus been unfaithful even to the slightest degree, he could never have uttered that confident request with the sure expectation that the Father would receive him. If he had disobeyed his Father's will, then he could not have said, "It is finished," nor have expected that the Father would and could receive him into his hands upon death. Nevertheless, Jesus knew that he had fulfilled the Scriptures and that he had finished the Father's will. In that confidence of his own righteousness, he could expect the glory afterward. Faithful Jesus was, right to the very end of his earthly life. Upon the basis of that faithfulness of Christ rests firmly our blessed atonement, redemption, and reconciliation to the Father!

This faithfulness continues to be one of the

outstanding virtues of the exalted Lord Jesus Christ. Jesus is called "the faithful witness" (Rev. 1:5). When he speaks to the angel of the church of the Laodiceans, Christ refers to himself as "the faithful and true witness" (Rev. 3:14). In Revelation 19:11, we see the exalted Christ sitting upon the white horse, and his name is "Faithful and True."

Why is it so important that we know that our exalted Lord is faithful?

First, because he did the will of the Father for our redemption in his death and resurrection in all faithfulness; we may be doubly sure that he continues at God's right hand to execute God's counsel for the establishment and fulfillment of his covenant in the same faithfulness. The gathering of his elect from the nations of the earth until his coming again shall surely come to pass. Of all that the Father has given to Christ from eternity, he shall lose not one. As many as God has ordained to eternal life shall believe, because Christ shall see to it that by his Spirit they will believe his gospel through the preaching of the gospel that he sovereignly directs and controls. All those that should be saved according to God's good pleasure shall be added to the church according to his timing and good wisdom.

Second, Christ has also revealed that as our heavenly high priest who prays for us, he will pray that our faith will not fail. He is our faithful high priest who intercedes for us continuously so that our faith fails not. That faithfulness of Christ is necessary lest we perish in our sin and unbelief. Without Christ's faithfulness we cannot believe and learn the faithful life of daily conversion and repentance at the foot of the cross of Christ and also learn a faithful life of godliness and honorable virtue. Without that prayer of Christ, by which we daily receive the grace and mercy for our salvation, we cannot have the beginning of the life of faithfulness to God. Christ's faithfulness makes the virtue of faithfulness for us, in us, and through us possible.

Christ's loyalty to his church is encouraging. Because he is faithful, he promised that he will be with his church unto the end. He will not forsake his people. He will not leave his sheep and lambs so that they are destroyed by the devil, by the world, or by themselves. He is our good shepherd, who provides his church with the necessary gifts and means to be preserved unto the end. All of the promises that Christ declares to his church are true, and he is faithful to them and to all those in whom those promises must be realized.

Because Christ is faithful to his church, his saints also share in that blessed virtue of faithfulness by his Spirit of sanctification. Some of the saints noted in the Bible for their faithfulness are Abraham (Neh. 9:8);

Moses (Num. 12:7; Heb. 3:5); Daniel (Dan. 6:4); Hanani (Neh. 7:2); Shelamiah the priest, Zadok the scribe, Pedaiah, and Hanan (Neh. 13:13); the Colossian saints in general (Col. 1:2–9), and Onesimus of the Colossian church in particular (Col. 4:9).

The Lord gives special attention to the need for this virtue among officebearers in his church. Ministers to whom are entrusted the faithful doctrines of God's word must be faithful (2 Tim. 2:2). A minister must be faithful so that at the end of his ministry in a particular congregation or mission field, or at the end of his life when ready to meet his righteous and merciful judge, he may confess his faithfulness to Christ, his truth, and his places of labor for him. Like the apostle Paul, he may confess: "I have fought a good fight, I have finished my course, I have kept the faith" (2 Tim. 4:7).

That virtue of faithfulness to God, Christ, his truth, and a godly walk of life is not required exclusively for the ministry of the word. It is also a necessary virtue for the offices of elder and of deacon. Upon installation into office, every elder and deacon must answer this question: "Whether ye promise, agreeably to said doctrine, faithfully, according to your ability, to discharge your respective offices?"[1] By their

---

[1] Form for Ordination of Elders and Deacons, in *Confessions and Church Order*, 292.

"Yes" in response and by their signature to the Formula of Subscription, they promise before Christ and his church and, consequently, over against the enemies of Christ and his church that they will "diligently teach and faithfully defend the aforesaid doctrine."[2] They pledge to be faithful to Christ and his church in their work for the duration of their term in office. Faithfulness in officebearers toward Christ and his word and faithfulness in their behaving orderly and decently in the church institute are necessary for the spiritual welfare and continuation of faithful churches.

Lest we overlook the wives of officebearers, the Lord reminds them of the need to be faithful: "Even so must their wives be grave, not slanderers, sober, faithful in all things" (1 Tim. 3:11). Just as important as it is for men to have the necessary qualifications for being deacons and elders, so also is it important that their wives be "faithful in all things"—to their husbands, to their homes, to their Lord, in all aspects of their station and calling in life. Their faithfulness will assist their husbands not to be weary in the well-doing of faithful labors in the churches.

Children must be faithful to their parents in all good and lawful things. The Heidelberg Catechism teaches children to show "all honor,

---

2 Formula of Subscription, in ibid, 326.

love, and fidelity" to their parents.[3] That fidelity is the same as faithfulness. Children must be faithful to submit to their parents and to obey them in all good and lawful things for the Lord's sake. Children are in duty bound to be faithful to the covenantal instruction of their parents, so that when the children are old they will in faithfulness not depart from the good instruction of their believing parents.

Workers must be faithful to their masters or employers (Eph. 6:5–8). They may not steal from their employers by wasting their time or abilities on company time, but be faithful. What is the purpose of that? The purpose is that the godly employee may adorn the doctrine of God in all things (Titus 2:9–10). That word to servants or workers reminds us that if one confesses the doctrines that are faithful to God's word, but does not adorn those doctrines with godliness, his confession and Reformed Christianity are vain and hollow. Faithfulness in our daily lives in the station and calling to employers, or others in positions of authority over us in the work place, shows our inner, heartfelt faithfulness to Christ and to our heavenly Father out of the motive of thankfulness.

The Scriptures teach that faithfulness is a virtue that we must desire for ourselves in ever richer measure. By way of contrast, we must detest the shamefulness of unfaithfulness. We

3 Heidelberg Catechism A 104, in ibid, 129.

are taught in Psalm 78 to set our hope in God, our faithful God, and not to be as the fathers, a stubborn and rebellious generation who set not their heart aright and whose spirit was not steadfast with God (Ps. 78:7–8). Later on in Psalm 78, the Lord shows how Israel was not steadfast with God and was unfaithful. Israel "tempted and provoked the most high God, and kept not his testimonies: But turned back, and dealt unfaithfully like their fathers: they were turned aside like a deceitful bow" (Ps. 78:56–57). For that unfaithfulness God severely judged Israel in the wilderness with forty years of chastisement in their wanderings. In Canaan during the days of the judges, when every man did what was right according to his own understanding and, as a result, became unfaithful to Jehovah, he sent severe judgments upon Israel's chronic unfaithfulness (Ps. 78:58–64).

Since God by his judgments upon Israel showed his hatred against her unfaithfulness, so must we hate unfaithfulness to Christ, hate disloyalty to God's truth, and hate quitting the way of laboring in our stations and callings in life by a true and living faith. Instead, marveling in the faithfulness of our God toward us in Christ Jesus and for his sake alone, let us be steadfast to him in cheerful contentment and in humble submission to his commandments and his wise way for our lives.

"Be thou faithful unto death, and I will give thee a crown of life," Christ commands and promises (Rev. 2:10). Living out of God's truth daily, praying on the basis of God's promises and his mercies, new every morning, and laboring daily through faith in Christ alone is the way of our faithfulness. In that way, we hear and delight in blessed promises of the crown of life and much more. He that is faithful shall not be hurt by the second death, which is hell (v. 11). Instead, in heaven he shall eat of the hidden manna, and he will receive a white stone with a new name written upon it (v. 17). He shall receive power over the nations and shall receive the morning star (vv. 27–28). He shall be clothed in white raiment. He shall know that his name is written in the Lamb's book of life (Rev. 3:4–5). He shall have the expectation of becoming a permanent pillar in the house of God and of receiving a new name (v. 12). Finally, he shall have the blessed expectation that he will sit with Christ in glory on his throne.

How sweet is this fruit of the Spirit and its results! The faithful labors and covenantal instruction of God-fearing parents yields, by the grace of God alone, the fruit of children who walk with their parents in the truth. The faithful labors of church officebearers yield the fruit, by the grace of God alone, of congregations that are built up and strengthened in the life and confession of the Reformed faith. The faithfulness of husband and wife to each other, until God by death separates them, yields the fruit of a stable, peaceful, Christ-centered, and God-glorifying home. The faithfulness of a believer to Jesus Christ throughout his life in his station and calling, even unto his last fleeting breath, yields the fruit of a crown of life. Upon wearing that crown of life, we may in eternal faithfulness praise our covenant God for his everlasting and never-failing mercies in Christ Jesus toward us, and in the perfection of that faithfulness know fully that Jehovah's faithfulness is incomparably great!

Questions for Discussion

1. How is the fruit of faithfulness important for holy marriage and for any godly friendship?

2. When is the activity of faithfulness especially important for church members and for officebearers in the church?

3. How should the faithfulness of God toward us inspire us unto faithfulness toward others?

4. In what ways are we prone to become weary in well-doing?

5. What is the blessed and motivating reward of grace for the activity of faithfulness?

Chapter 9

MEEKNESS

A virtue that the Holy Spirit nurtures in the believer by the doctrines of his sovereign, electing, and irresistible grace is the virtue of meekness. The Canons of Dordt teach that "the sense and certainty of this election afford to the children of God additional matter for daily humiliation before Him."[1] In the Canons of Dordt we confess that the doctrine of the preservation and perseverance of the saints does not produce in the believer a "spirit of pride," but is "a source of humility," among many other worthy virtues.[2] These statements imply that humility, or meekness, is vital to the Christian life, and it is a fruit of the Spirit of Christ in us that he nurtures by means of the faithful preaching of God's sovereign, electing grace in Christ Jesus alone.

---

1 Canons of Dordt, 1.13, in *Confessions and Church Order*, 157

2 Canons of Dordt, 5.12, in ibid, 175.

Meekness was prominent in the lives of God's saints in Scripture. For example, according to Numbers 12:3, "Moses was very meek, above all the men which were upon the face of the earth." Although he was not sinless in this life, which became evident in his sin at Kadeshbarnea, yet the Lord worked in Moses the virtue of meekness to a very great extent. John the Baptist showed meekness when he confessed that he was not even worthy to unloose the buckles on the shoes of Jesus (John 1:27) and when he confessed to his disciples that he wanted himself to decrease and Jesus to increase (John 3:30). Paul showed the virtue of meekness when in 1 Timothy 1:15 he confessed that "Christ Jesus came into the world to save sinners; of whom I am chief."

From these examples we learn that this virtue must be present and prominent in our hearts. For example, in 1 Peter 3:4 wives are admonished to adorn themselves with the beauty of a meek and quiet spirit, and to value that jewel and beautiful adornment as God values it: of great price! Believers must exercise humility when restoring in mercy one in the church who has fallen into sin. This they must do in the spirit of meekness, considering themselves, lest they also be tempted and fall, from pride, into great sin (Gal. 6:1). We learn in Philippians 2:2–4 that meekness, or humility, is necessary for the continued enjoyment of the communion of saints in the church. As Christ was humble, and demonstrated that humility in his work of redemption, so must we be of the same mind and in that lowliness of mind esteem others better than ourselves.

Opposite to that is selfishness. Thinking of me first and only about me is not humility. The Lord teaches in Philippians 2:4: "Look not every man on his own things, but every man also on the things of others." Selfishness for one's own name and glory is the enemy of humility, especially in cases where the honor of God's name is at stake. The truly humble will stand up and face the heat of the battle against the dishonor of God's name or become very vocal for the faith when it is attacked in pernicious ways by the devil and false teachers. Meek Moses did not stand by idly when the people worshiped the golden calf at Mount Sinai. On the Lord's side, meek Moses took swift action to put an end to such evil in the camp. However, the selfish will avoid such battles.

The opposite of humility is vainglory. One who falls into the trap of vainglory seeks the praise and honor of men in order to puff up his esteem of himself. He seeks to build his self-esteem on himself, his own works, and his own goodness. Vainglory and self-esteem are a deadly trap that draws us away from Christ, whose all-sufficient worth is imputed to us by faith alone.

The enemy of humility is pride. Pride can become a sin in church members when they behave with haughtiness toward others who have not been called and converted, as though they by their own abilities made themselves to differ. Pride was the sin of the Pharisee who prayed in thanksgiving to his god that he was so much better than others, especially the publican in the same parable that Jesus taught in Luke 18. Pride can also be manifest in a refusal to turn away from any false teaching, from a wicked walk of life, from an offense committed against others, or from a very unwise and potentially harmful direction or decision in life. Pride can become manifest in one who thinks that God has not given him enough gifts to serve in his particular station and calling in life. Such a conclusion is a manifestation of pride against the God of wisdom, who distributes his gifts to his people with perfect precision and then commands them to use those abilities in humble dependence upon the Lord in their specific station and calling.

Pride can easily become manifest in feeling sorry for ourselves when calamities in life strike. When one feels sorry for himself, he has not humbled himself before the mighty hand of God, who gives not only our calamities and afflictions in life, but also provides the grace sufficient each day to endure the trials of life with patience and godly fear (1 Pet. 5:6–7).

Pride becomes manifest when one becomes like Elijah and thinks that he is the only one left who cares and stands for the truth of God's word, while everyone else is unregenerated, unconverted, or on the road to apostasy. Such forget that God does have his seven thousand preserved by his grace. Pride is manifest when we begin to think that we, of ourselves, are better and more worthy than others for whatever reason.

Instead of those evil virtues, the child of God must desire to have and exercise the fruit of meekness. Philippians 2:3 describes meekness clearly: "lowliness of mind." Meekness is a matter of how lowly we value ourselves—before God chiefly and also in comparison with others. In meekness one concludes that before God he is only an undeserving servant, and in comparison with others he is the least of the least of all God's saints. That conclusion is not a putting down of oneself before others with false motives, but a genuine understanding that he is the least of the least of God's saints because he is the chief of the chief of sinners. When we understand how huge and extensive our sin and misery are, we will understand how low we really are. Then we will understand how great God and Christ are, that we are as nothing before God, and in comparison to others we are far below the lowest. Then the Spirit makes us to see that the worth we do have is of, in, by, and because of Christ alone. He is our wisdom, righteousness, sanctification, and redemption entirely.

As is true of all the other aspects of the fruit of the Spirit, we do not possess true meekness naturally. That fact does not take long to appear in us as we grow up. In early childhood already one expresses effortlessly and naturally selfishness and pride as he rips away a toy from another child or refuses to obey his parent and to come when called. True humility before God and in relationship to God is truly a gift of God's grace, worked in us by the Holy Spirit alone. God must crush our rock-hard hearts by his grace and give us new hearts that are pliable and soft. He must infuse in us the life and mind of Christ, who said, "For I am meek and lowly in heart" (Matt. 11:29). In fact, Christ was so lowly and meek that he came into our flesh in the way of his lowly birth, to walk a lowly way of humiliation, to the lowliest depths of hell, for the lowliest of all, his own sheep, who also by nature hate, reject, and would crucify him again.

It is humbling, is it not, that Christ humbled himself so low for us in order that we, who deserve to be cast down, might inhabit the heights of undeserved glory in his heavenly kingdom? What Christ by his death and resurrection earned for us, a life of his humility, he is pleased to work in us by his Spirit through the preaching of the word. By the preaching of the gospel of God's sovereign, electing grace in Christ, the Spirit is pleased to call us out of the darkness and death of pride into the light and life of genuine humility.

That virtue we need for faithful lives in our respective churches, homes, and places in daily life. For example, the meek wife will be faithful to her husband in her lifelong marriage, will guide her house with wisdom and discretion, and also, as time and opportunity permit, bear the burdens of others within the household of faith.

With this virtue the Christian young person can attain the proper estimation of himself before God and in comparison to others. He will see his nothingness apart from Christ and will resist the death-trap of seeking value for himself in his own report card grades, in his diplomas, in his successful school or work projects, and in his friends. He will see that his all is in Christ alone and, in thanksgiving for that, faithfully go to school, find employment, seek a like-minded spouse, make confession of faith, and mature in the obligations of church membership.

With this virtue, lasting spiritual friendships at various levels in life are maintained. The friendship of Jonathan and David is an example of how the blessing of humility is vital to the happy friendships of fellow believers, even in extremely difficult circumstances.

In such relationships in life, the meek look out for the spiritual welfare of the others. The meek will not behave independently and individualistically. They will not say, "I am not my brother's keeper." They will not even build their home independently from the homes of fellow believers and their seed. They will not say that the children of other believers are not their concern. This does not mean that the meek will fall into the opposite error of being busybodies, intermeddling in the affairs of others in which they have no place, and at the same time leaving their own calling and duties unfinished. Rather, the meek will be ready to serve others as time and opportunity permit because of a deep spiritual concern and interest for the spiritual health of other believers and their seed.

As the meek fulfill their callings in the church, home, and other areas of life, they put others first. The husband will think of his wife first, and so the wife toward her husband. The meek parents will not put themselves, their vacations, their hobbies, or other earthly desires first, but will put the needs and spiritual welfare of their children and their children's children first. Bearing the burdens of fellow saints becomes a priority for the meek. Interceding for others in the church in prayer before God's throne of grace is a daily element of the prayers of the meek. Just as the Father in heaven so esteemed those others in the church that he gave his only begotten Son for them, so surely must we esteem our fellow saints.

This virtue would not be present in us except there also abides in us the love of Christ. Like all the other aspects of the fruit of the Spirit, meekness also flows out of the first part of the fruit of the Spirit: love. Love is that bond of perfectness, the bond of covenant communion with God in which we seek him first only because he has sought us first. When Christ pours into us his love by his Spirit, we love him. When there is that love of Christ in us, we will hate the world and the evils of pride and delight ourselves in his life of meekness. With the love of Christ in our hearts we will learn to live in humility before God and in relationships with other people. By the love of Christ, we will be longsuffering, kind, good, and faithful toward others.

What is the result of meekness? In this life there is, according to Psalm 37:11, something wonderful that the meek may enjoy. David wrote that the meek "shall delight themselves in the abundance of peace." The result of true humility is the enjoyment of an abundance of peace, which surpasses our understanding, with our fellow saints and, above all, with our God through our Lord Jesus Christ.

According to Psalm 37:11, the meek may also expect to "inherit the earth." Jesus repeated that in the Beatitudes: "Blessed are the meek: for they shall inherit the earth" (Matt. 5:5). The blessed hope and expectation for the meek, though they are persecuted and oppressed in this life, is that they shall one day soon be highly exalted into their place in the everlasting and heavenly kingdom of Christ.

Questions for Discussion

1. Is constant self-deprecation the same as meekness? Is always keeping quiet and being shy the same as meekness?

2. How does meekness affect our evaluation of others?

3. How is finding our worth in what we do and who we are an enemy to true meekness?

4. When does it become especially difficult to be meek toward others?

5. What things are necessary for us to have in order to develop in humility and meekness?

Chapter 10

TEMPERANCE

The last aspect of the fruit of the Spirit is the virtue of temperance. Temperance is more commonly known as self-control or self-discipline. Another word similar to temperance is *modesty*.

This virtue is not mentioned often in the Bible, in comparison to some of the other aspects of the fruit of the Spirit. It is mentioned seven times in the New Testament. Included among the seven references is its use in Acts 24:25, where it refers to how a governor should rule well and live in view of the coming day of the Lord in his judgment. In 1 Corinthians 7:9, the apostle Paul mentions temperance in connection with the single life, sex, and marriage. Paul wrote, "But if they cannot contain [be temperate], let them marry: for it is better to marry than to burn." In Titus 1:8, temperance is listed as one of the qualifications for the office of elder. Another example of the use of temperance in the New Testament is 2 Peter 1:5–6. There Peter admonishes, "Add to your faith virtue; and to virtue knowledge; and to knowledge temperance; and to temperance patience; and to patience godliness." Our knowledge of the Lord and of his truth must be coupled closely with virtue on the one side and temperance on the other.

Finally, in 1 Corinthians 9:24–27, Paul wrote about the importance of temperance in his own life and work as an apostle. "And every man that striveth for the mastery is temperate in all things. Now they do it to obtain a corruptible crown; but we an incorruptible" (v. 25). If temperance is vital for the success of a worldly athlete for the prize of an Olympic gold medal, should it not be regarded by us as more than vital for the prize for which we press forward by faith? That it ought to be highly valued by the believer is emphasized by Paul when he writes, "But I keep under my body, and bring it into subjection: lest that by any means, when I have preached to others, I myself should be a castaway" (1 Cor. 9:27).

The temperance that the apostle Paul needed in his own life and apostolic labors is illustrated in 1 Corinthians 9:26 by two familiar examples. The Olympic marathon runner or sprinter competed in races with the desire to win the prize of the winner's wreath. However, to obtain that championship prize, the marathon runner or sprinter had to train extensively and prepare both his body and mind to race for victory. In like manner, after training himself vigorously and extensively both mentally and physically for the grueling matches, the boxer competes in the ring with explosive intensity, meticulously honed reflexes, and a deliberate strategy in order to obtain the championship belt. Both types of athletes do everything necessary, governing all aspects of their life, mind, and body meticulously, in order to obtain the sole objective of the gold medal or championship belt.

Similarly, the apostle explained that it was necessary for him to be so governed in all areas of his life that he could be effective in his work for the welfare of the church. All distractions and hindrances had to be rejected and resolutely avoided. He was required to keep even his body under control so that the church would be faithfully served. Without temperance, the apostle would have been at best like a shadow-boxer, one beating on thin air or beating on the wrong opponent; or like a marathon runner who runs in the wrong direction or runs off course onto an illegal shortcut, because of which he is disqualified. Without temperance Paul would have been an unfaithful preacher and the welfare of the church put in jeopardy.

In light of the apostle's instruction, we may understand that temperance for the officebearer and the believer alike is that spiritual ability to bring themselves under control for godly and faithful lives unto the Lord. Temperance is the inner strength to be a master over oneself and to be ruled with a Christ-centered purpose in life. One who is temperate does not let himself become a slave to whim, uncontrolled passions, the deceitfulness of riches, carnal lusts, or other evils, such as peer-pressure. One who is temperate puts himself under such control, that whatever good and profitable thing he must desire to do, that is the godly thing that he pursues by faith.

Temperance is the ability to govern oneself completely in all circumstances of life. Temperance is the virtue that applies to times of ease and times of crisis; times of wealth and times of poverty; times of health and times of sickness; and times when one is full of ambitious energy and times when at the end of the day one is thoroughly drained. Temperance in those situations is to have spiritual control over ourselves so that we continue in the life of godliness, love, and thankfulness to our heavenly Father.

This virtue applies to so many things in our lives, including even our use of time. Are you temperate or disciplined with your use of the gift of time? Do you make time for significant prayer each day with God? Do you make time for Scripture?

Temperance applies to our daily bread. Are we temperate with our food: eating in moderation?

Are we, in our warfare against this present Sodom-like world, abstaining from using the gift of sex in the single life, and faithfully using the gift of sex in the marriage bond, in obedience to God's seventh commandment and his ordinance of the one-flesh union of marriage?

In that regard, are we temperate even in what we allow our eyes to see? (Ps. 101:3).

According to 2 Peter 1:6, true temperance is joined closely to virtue, faith, and knowledge. True temperance arises out of a regenerated heart of faith, aims for the eternal and spiritual value of God's glory, and is full of the knowledge of God, Christ, particular redemption, the commandments of the Lord, and a life motivated by thanksgiving to God. True temperance aims at the prize of covenantal fellowship with the Father in heavenly glory in the way of faithful and thankful service to him.

For that prize and for our salvation and redemption, Christ was temperate. In opposition to Christ's resolute discipline to fulfill all righteousness for us in love to God, Satan tempted Jesus in the wilderness to turn the nearby stones into bread. Though he had been without food for forty days, Christ kept his body in subjection and did not permit his aching stomach to determine how he would respond to Satan. In his defense against and victory over the devil, Christ declared authoritatively from Scripture, "Man shall not live by bread

alone, but by every word that proceedeth out
of the mouth of God" (Matt. 4:4). Throughout
his ministry, Christ had perfect self-discipline
and self-control. When rejected by the people of
Nazareth at the cliff's edge and turning toward
the unbelieving multitude to walk through
the midst of them, Jesus did not call down fire
from heaven to burn them all up. Instead, he
bore the reproach and rejection of wicked men
as part of the accursed way that he was required
to walk for our full redemption.

Because of Christ's redemption the temperance of Christ is given to us as a sovereignly-
worked gift of the Spirit of our Lord. Of course,
true temperance is not naturally present in us.
Daily our sins in many ways show that we do
not govern ourselves very well in the service
of the Lord. By nature we are intemperate and
prone to excess in self in many ways. Hence
true temperance is a miraculous work of God's
grace in and through us.

Bringing ourselves under the regulation of
Christ and his word makes us realize that
the words *self-government, self-control,* or *self-
discipline* might be misleading. He who is truly
temperate does not wish to be governed by his
self. The Spirit of Christ teaches us to be willing
and ready to live in submission unto him.
Although temperance is the ability to govern
all of our bodily and spiritual members in a
harmonious choir of thanksgiving to God all

the days of our lives, yet ultimately temperance is the spiritual ability to be governed willingly by Christ's word and Spirit. Temperance delights to be bound by Christ's yoke, which is easy and light. Temperance delights to be a citizen of Christ's kingdom and under his government of grace. True temperance flourishes in the Christian's liberty of being bound entirely by the government of Christ.

As you can readily understand, this temperance does not mean an easy life. It was not so for Paul. Likewise, the temperate believer must live a life of self-denial, and he must war daily against his intemperate old nature. He must expect to face persecution from the unbelieving world. For example, he will be mocked by worldly fellow workers as they head off to the night club or neighborhood pub after a long day of work, and he heads home to the needs of his wife and children. The temperate believer will be mocked by his worldly, fun-loving neighbors because he and his godly wife must closely regulate their use of money for the support of the church, the poor, their family, and the Christian school. The temperate Christian young woman and young man will be mocked when they in temperance reject the world's temptations to flaunt their sexuality by immodesty in dress and in dance with or in front of the opposite sex. In spite of the many difficulties that the spiritually temperate must face while living in a world intoxicated with carnal self-indulgence, if this virtue of temperance, along with the other virtues of the fruit of the Spirit, be in them, they will be neither unfruitful nor barren branches in the knowledge of the Lord Jesus Christ.

There is for the temperate believer the encouraging hope of a worthy crown of glory at life's end because of God's grace in Christ Jesus. Athletes today pursue corruptible crowns. Being corruptible, they and their earthly glory will all perish, either in this life already under God's curse, or most certainly in the great fire and destruction upon the earth and creation when the Lord in his final appearing will make all things of the earthly creation new and heavenly. However, for the truly temperate in Christ there is that better crown that does not fade in its glory and value. Having in spiritual modesty and discipline finished his course, fought the good fight, and reached the finish line of his work and life, the apostle could be confident that the Lord would give him in grace a beautiful crown (2 Tim. 4:7–8). Ought not we in holy temperance pursue such a crown from the Lord whom we love?

May the Spirit of our Lord by his almighty and sanctifying grace make us fruitful branches in Christ Jesus, so that we may bring forth the fruit of the Spirit abundantly and in all its spiritual sweetness to the glory of God triune and to the praise of his wondrous grace.

Questions for Discussion

1. How does the fruit of temperance affect our attitude toward earthly things?

2. In what areas of your life do you sometimes lack temperance and self-control?

3. How does the world promote self-indulgence and so tempt the believer?

4. What connection does the first commandment have with temperance?

5. Upon what goal must the believer focus in this virtue of temperance?

Chapter 11

CONCLUSION

There are a few thoughts from Scripture that are worth considering as a conclusion to the examination of the fruit of the Spirit.

First, the presence and growth of the fruit of the Spirit is rooted and grounded in election. Election is described by the Canons of Dordt as "the fountain of every saving good," including all the gifts of salvation.[1] This means that the fruit of the Spirit is found only in the elect, but never in the reprobate, however civilized they may be outwardly. In those whom God does not intend to save, there can be no fruit of the Spirit present. Only in his precious elect in Christ, and in those alone, will the fruit of the Spirit be wonderfully brought forth by his sovereign grace alone.

What the Canons of Dordt declare regarding election and its fruits is firmly grounded in

---

1 Canons of Dordt, 1.9, in *Confessions and Church Order*, 157.

Scripture's revelation of election. For example, that statement is based upon Romans 8:29, "For whom he did foreknow, he also did predestinate to be conformed unto the image of his Son, that he might be the firstborn among many brethren."

In connection with the fruit of the Spirit, this text speaks of the saving work of God whereby he conforms us into the image of his Son. He raises us out of the death of sin and works in us the new life of Christ. We are transformed into the image of Christ so that more and more we look like him and behave like him. That image is the living reflection of the life and virtues of Christ. It is the shining forth of the light of Christ from within our regenerated hearts. That light is seen within us by the fruit of the Spirit.

Romans 8:29 reveals that the work of God to transform us into the image of Christ so that we become a living reflection of his blessed virtues is rooted in election. God willed from before the foundation of the world that we would possess the life and virtues of Christ so that in the last day Christ might have around him many glorified brethren in the heavenly family of God.

The benefit of the connection between election and the fruit of the Spirit is twofold. On the one hand, it assures the believer that this good pleasure of God, that determines that we must receive and enjoy this beautiful task of the bringing forth the fruit of the Spirit, cannot be and will not be interrupted, changed, recalled, or annulled. This assures us that although we are not yet delivered from the infirmities of our flesh or from the body of sin, wherein is a source of great discouragement, yet our election and its final outcome in the coming day of our Lord Jesus Christ is sure. This gives us unspeakable consolation in life and death.

On the other hand, this election unto the virtues of the fruit of the Spirit affords us much reason for daily humiliation before God. In light of who we are now, this election and its fruit keep us utterly amazed at the mercies of God toward us and motivate us unto daily thankfulness and love to God, who first revealed such great love toward us.[2]

Second, the Holy Spirit is pleased to work his fruit in the heart and life of the regenerated child of God in connection with the preaching of the word of God, also known as the chief means of grace. It is not to be expected that the production of the fruit of the Spirit is an automatic process in which we are completely inactive and need not expend any energy nor exert any effort. It is not to be expected that below or beyond our consciousness the fruit of the Spirit suddenly appears in our lives.

On the contrary, the Lord works the fruit of

---

2 Canons of Dordt, 1.13, in ibid, 157.

the Spirit in us through the rigorous process of sanctification and preservation. Just as the husbandman rigorously and faithfully prunes his vines so that the branches produce the best grapes and in abundant quantities, so the Lord faithfully prunes his living branches. Through suffering, trials, much prayer, and normally a lifetime of instruction and admonition through the preaching of the word, the child of God is pruned in order to bring forth good fruit and more fruit. There are examples in the Bible of this work of God by means in the lives of God's saints. Each example is a reminder of exactly how God is pleased to prune his children in this life so that what he has eternally willed and surely promised may, in fact, become a reality in their hearts and lives.

As a result, it is necessary that we subject ourselves to the God-ordained means by which we are saved. For the faithful and continuous production of the fruit of the Spirit and our growth in that daily activity, we must, for example, faithfully attend the means of grace. We are obligated to be active and faithful confessing members of a faithful congregation where the word of God is preached faithfully and purely. This truth is summarized by the Canons of Dordt: "And as it hath pleased God, by the preaching of the gospel, to begin this work of grace in us, so He preserves, continues, and perfects it by the hearing and the reading of His Word, by meditation thereon, and by the exhortations, threatenings, and promises thereof, as well as by the use of the sacraments."[3]

Under the means of grace, Christ works in and through us the fruit of the Spirit. In fact, the preaching of the word by the working of the Spirit has the powerful effect in the elect and regenerated child of God of a good change. Two Corinthians 3:18 speaks of this amazing spiritual change: "But we all, with open face beholding as in a glass the glory of the Lord, are changed into the same image from glory to glory, even as by the Spirit of the Lord." While we look at the glorious virtues of Christ revealed through the mirror of the preaching of Christ crucified and risen, the shining light of them are by the Spirit worked in us. What we see in the mirror of God's word concerning Christ, is exactly what the Lord mysteriously and graciously begins to make to appear in us. While this positive change may be hardly noticeable to us at times, yet 2 Corinthians 3:18 assures us that the word of God is the power of God that works in us slowly, but surely, the glory of salvation more and more, including the production of the fruit of the Spirit.

Third, we are compelled by the Lord to understand that in the fruit of the Spirit is true freedom.

---

3   Canons of Dordt, 5.14, in ibid, 176.

The believer is frequently bombarded with the worldly temptations that declare to him that true freedom is found in deliverance from the strict rules of God's commandments and in the pursuit of our own corrupt wills and self-centered wants, under the guidance of unbridled lust. The life of Christ is declared to be a miserable bondage, and the pursuit of sin is declared to be real happiness and freedom. The power of the drama, with all its powerfully impressive visual and audio effects, the power of attractive advertisements, and the power of worldly music all shout that the way of wickedness is the only "good life." Often we face the evil attractiveness and allure of the ways of disobedience. By sight and according to outward observation and according to human wisdom, it does appear that to be selfish, to be free of the yoke of Christ, and to do all the works of the flesh are real freedom.

However, all that is opposed to God and the Holy Spirit is not life, but only death and lies under God's curse. Against all that temptation offers there is the law: "You shall not." As soon as we disobey, there is death. In fact, we are warned sharply that all those who continue in such sins "shall not inherit the kingdom of God" (Gal. 5:21). Rather, they shall earn for themselves an everlasting prison of shame and death in hell.

In contrast, after revealing the nine aspects of

the fruit of the Spirit, Galatians 5:23 concludes with the truth that true freedom and happiness is found in the fruit of the Spirit. With regard to freedom and happiness in all of the aspects of the fruit of the Spirit, "against such there is no law." As far as the fruit of the Spirit is concerned, there are no restrictions and oppressive regulations. Our true freedom is to flourish abundantly in the fruit of the Spirit unto the glory of God. The reality that this is our true freedom will become fully revealed when we inherit the everlasting kingdom of God in heaven and bring forth the fruit of the Spirit perfectly. Hence let this truth in Galatians 5:23 motivate us daily to seek the grace and strength of Christ to bring forth the fruit of the Spirit in thanksgiving to God. In that way we enjoy the freedom of sanctified and holy lives.

Fourth, we may not forget, lest we boast in ourselves or trust in ourselves, that our lives and growth in the fruit of the Spirit are entirely dependent upon Christ. Christ has given us the legal right to this position of the bringing forth of the fruit of the Spirit on the basis of his death on the cross. Christ is also the living power to raise us out of the death of sin and unbelief into his new life of love, joy, peace, longsuffering, gentleness, goodness, faithfulness, meekness, and temperance.

It is good to remember each day what Jesus said in John 15:1–8, especially these words: "for without me ye can do nothing." Indeed, without Christ we can do nothing, except bring forth the rotten and bitter fruits of sin, unbelief, and death. Only because of him, by him, and in him can we through his indwelling Spirit have this new life of the sweet fruit of the Holy Spirit.

Finally, the Lord gives us the blessed hope of the coming day when we shall attain perfection in the fruit of the Spirit. We who must fight daily against the weakness of our sinful flesh may well wonder if that day is even possible. Yet, the Scriptures declare firmly that the day is coming. When the number of the elect is complete and the Lord appears in his glory with his holy angels in his glorious, final, and bodily appearing, we shall then be made like him. Of this hope, speaks 1 John 3:2: "Beloved, now are we the sons of God, and it doth not yet appear what we shall be: but we know that, when he shall appear, we shall be like him; for we shall see him as he is." We shall be like him fully in many things, but particularly like him in the perfection of his virtues of the fruit of the Spirit. Then we shall enjoy the fullness of the fruit of the Spirit without any spot of sin or unbelief.

Of course, we shall partake of that perfection when after this life we are received up into glory with the Lord. Yet, we shall partake of it in its fullest glory and purpose when finally we are received into the complete assembly of the resurrected and glorified saints and of the angels in life everlasting.

Let us then pray that life and growth in the fruit of the Spirit be worked and preserved in his saints in this life. Let that which the world of wicked men utterly despise and detest in its small beginning in the Lord's beloved saints in this life flourish completely, without interruption, in full victory over the kingdom of darkness and in the everlasting and holy communion of the saints and angels in life everlasting with our Lord.

Questions for Discussion

1. How does affliction and suffering affect our bringing forth the fruit of the Spirit?

2. How should the truth of the fruit of the Spirit affect the instruction of the covenant youth?

3. How does the truth of the fruit of the Spirit help people of God to discover and to develop friendships?

4. In terms of the fruit of the Spirit, what is true freedom for the believer? In what ways does the world contradict this truth?

5. In what ways is the believer's hope of perfection in the fruit of the Spirit certain?

Notes